AGENDA 2021,
The New World Order, One World Babylon

ESCAPING THIS
COMING DESCTRUCTION
Through

BIBLE
CODE 7

Agenda 2021,
The New World Order, One World Babylon
**BIBLE PROPHECIED DESTRUCTION OF BABYLON U.S.A.
END TIMES TRIBULATION WARNINGS**

Dr. Norman Dacosta

Xulon Press

Xulon Press
2301 Lucien Way #415
Maitland, FL 32751
407.339.4217
www.xulonpress.com

Printed in the United States of America.

Paperback ISBN-13: 9781632214133
eBook ISBN-13: 9781632214140

Table of Contents

Foreword

My father Harold DaCosta left me a great legacy, not money, but a prophetic statement of urgency to propel me forward in life and fulfill my God given destiny. A very hard working man with a great work ethic, who loved and respected people, so love and respect came back to him, what he sowed he reaped. Just before he passed away, on one of my visits to the hospice care facility where he was, he exclaimed to me in a lamenting tone, Ah my son,

"<u>Too late we learn, and too soon we die</u>". This prophetic statement is my Dad's legacy to me.

Thank you Dad.

My mother Clutilder was a take no trash, no nonsense warrior, a housekeeper for a very wealthy family, but no one could belittle, berate or disrespect her, she gave respect and demanded by her demeanor and lifestyle kindness respect in return. A tough as nails determination, take no nonsense from anybody, no matter how rich, a woman whose spiritual DNA I inherited. **Thank you Mom.**

Hatred is not found or based in the code of men, the DNA, but is based in the soul of individuals, the inner recesses of the heart. Hatred is an emotion, just as love is also an emotion that comes from the soul, the heart. The Bible declares that, 'the heart of man is deceitful and above all things desperately wicked and who knows it?' No one but Jesus. The inner recesses of the mind harbors dangerous thoughts and imaginations.

The heart is controlled or governed by either the Spirit of the Lord or by demons under satan's control, it's either or, one or the other.

Feelings of superiority, supremacy and many other like feelings emanates from this seat of the hidden heart, and after multiple generations such thoughts will still manifest itself as something being deserved, or owed to one because of a privileged or deserved status. This describes the perpetuation of royalty, nobility, the ruling class. Feelings of such are now believed to become a right because of one's peerage, breeding or ancestry. Whenever wicked deceitful hearts band together, nothing but sheer evil will ensue, as satan the master engineer, is in the drivers seat.

Is such a person as this salvageable? Can they be pulled out of that pit of error? The answer is yes, but only with the help of destination engineer Jesus Christ.

Nations founded and run upon such rabid prejudiced beliefs will be wracked with strife as a certain class of people will arise and deem themselves to be the holders and owners of the reigns of their society because of their social breeding, peerage and membership in the clubs of power.

As this has been allowed to exist for generations, this has become the norm as the ruling class ten percenters of the world seeks to maintain the status quo of the rich ruling over the poor, with a layer of enforcer class people just below them, who are given more money and privileges than the masses to do their bidding, and so the status quo is maintained. The laws of the land are written by and for the benefit of the ruling class.

Media and all social platforms and formats are being used to benefit these rulers. Hidden deep undercover but in plain sight is the use of Baalamic or Simonic sorcery to keep the masses in bewitchment, delusion and bondage, a standard practice for the rich to do.

The world is filled with secret society groups too numerous to mention and hidden in plain sight, as the best place to hide something is in the very open, in plain sight and open view, so the ruling class never looks or seems like the monsters that they truly are. Some of the very best hiding places are in groups with noble sounding names and mission statements. The Club of Rome, Council on Foreign Relations, Bilderbergers, Black Nobility, Red Brigades, Freemasons, Royal Institute of International Affairs, Trilateral Commission etc. The most monstrous evils in the whole world is hidden in many of theses secret organizations with lofty sounding names but with the same biblical agenda which is,**"Prov. 22 vs. 7:The rich rules over the Poor and the borrower is the slave to the lender,"**. A one world government with the mark of the beast in every person without which no one can buy or sell is their final solution (Revelation 13 vs. 16). A 'surplus population' removal is now being planned and implemented by these murderous groups to destroy and trim the world's population by billions to about 500 million people to be ideally manageable for them. A scarcity of resources, food, potable water among other things is developing on the earth right now and a fierce jostling for scarce resources will ensue shortly, which will lead to bloody disastrous wars.

The very wealthy are very scared about an uprising against their satanic oppressive rule. Many are very secretive and are hiding in plain sight, unknown names, addresses and never a mention of them in the media.

The scared wealthy will then seek to lash out with more security guards, barriers, devices, gated fortresslike communities. In the near future, the levels of the well paid enforcer class mercenaries will increase drastically, and they will begin to work with a commando style zeal to bring about more security for the ruling class, and against the masses. Protection with powerful weapons and hi tech devices will be employed to the max. Note the security details of the very rich and the royals, how they have grown larger, more well equipped and armed.

However the wrong weapons are being used to fight in this battle by the masses, and taking ownership of this battle is the completely wrong strategy. Superior mighty weapons through God, fasting, His WORDS, from on high are available to those who believe in Jesus and must be employed and utilized constantly to destroy injustices and oppressions, not guns and physical means. Once these weapons are utilized, God takes over the battle, He owns it, it becomes His and He will never lose any battle given unto Him, He will fight for us, and the Word warriors will rest peacefully. Bloody and deceitful men will never live out half their days.

Man makes their plans, but God erases those plans and brings in a better plan, for of His Kingdom there shall be no end.

There is a blatant attempt to separate the Christian believers, to break their Church going habit, to quell the Churches, a persecution if you will has begun because the Church of Jesus Christ will not play ball with the evil agendas of the wicked ruling class. The first Amendment has been recently destroyed by the U.S. Supreme Court in their 5-4 ruling against the Church. They have begun to persecute Jesus Christ and He will surely meet them on the Damascus Road.

All these chaotic events occurring today coincide with the 'hidden in plain sight' master plan of 1992, the U.N. Sustainable Development Conference, of Rio De Janeiro Brazil June 3-14, 1992.

AGENDA 21. This master plan (351 pages) was accepted by 178 nations and the goals were set for a 10 year plan beginning in 2021 to last till 2030.

To kick off this plan on time beginning January 2021, is the reason for all this chaos occurring worldwide, for out of chaos, order must come. The ruling class ten percenters, will cause a living hell environment here on earth, especially in the USA, as the USA has the largest GDP, is the most affluent society and the last bastion of Christian faith and freedom. This hellish nightmare of chaos in the world will cause the masses to beg for someone, a hero, a savior to come and save them and the people from these hellish conditions. Then the new world order <u>GLOBAL</u> solutions of AGENDA 2021 will be offered, displayed and implemented. Again, according to their timetable, this master plan must be kicked off in 2021.

In 2021 this master plan is scheduled to begin, so to put the NEW world order in place, they must first destroy the OLD established world order. In the latter half of the year 2020, the beginning of the destruction of the old begins, and all who do not go along with the program will be marginalized, targeted for persecution and destruction by the satanic globalists.

Many will die, corralled, persecuted, great destruction will occur, great losses of money, properties and material possessions are coming. A crash and burn if you will. Destroy the old, replace with their new world order.

A hiding place will be desperately sought by all men. But those who are firm believers in Jesus are already hidden safe in Him;

Acts 17:28

28 For in him we live, and move, and have our being; as certain also of your own poets have said, For we are also his offspring.

Jesus therefore becomes our safety destination, our only hiding place while living here on earth. It now becomes our duty to remain in Him and in due time, He will translate us to our final destination to be with Him for all eternity.

Other Books By Dr. Norman Dacosta

@biblecode7.com
email drnormandacosta@gmail.com
Amazon
Barnes and Nobles.
iBooks
ebooks
kindle

Chapter 1

God's Weighing Of A Nation.

Tower of Babel
Babylon 1, the origin of Babylon worship

Shinar = Babylonia, Chaldea.

od created mankind in His image and after His likeness, this makes us very near and dear to Him, It is His will that all mankind should repent and embrace Jesus Christ so He can call us sons, or children, without this we cannot be called children of God, only His creation. After this has occurred, then His relation to us would be that of a Father. God desires faith in Him, obedience and trust from us. These desires of God from us are very reasonable considering the benefits we will reap from Him.

The very first worship service of a group of men that would defy the presence and authority of God was now about to be ushered in, in the plains of a place called Shinar, (Babylon), a city designed and built for satan's worship. This first satanic church gathering was pastored and led by Noah's grandson Nimrod. (Genesis 11). This was a gathering of seasoned people who were willing to be led and to do as all men desires to do out of a built in nature, that is to worship. This worship service took a different tone and turn however, as this was not a bless God worship service, but an anti God worship service where the Preacher Nimrod, (referred to as Apollo, or Abbadon in the New Testament Book of Revelation), Noah's grandson and congregants decided to build a tower to reach up to the very heavens and assault the very throne of God in the heavens, an observatory if you will, a very high place of worship to lift up their god upon and make sacrifices, but that god was not The Almighty God Jehovah, but none other than satan, the deceiver. This was to be an observatory to observe, worship and serve satan by worshipping the host of heaven, the heavenly bodies. Anywhere and everywhere satan shows up, he corrupts, perverts and destroys as he is not able to create but only rob, kill, destroy.

These Babylon worship services was involving all manner of sexual perversion, bestiality, immoralities, cannibalism, pedophilia, baby and human blood sacrifices as is the nature of satan to pervert and destroy. Sacrifices was of children offered up to their god moloch.

This is the first Babylon worship, the worship of satan in a perverted and demoralizing manner and casting God aside. This place Shinar means- Babylon, and very well remembered as the Tower of Babel which they began to build.

God's punishment- confusion of their languages, here we have the breakup of one language that all mankind spoke into the many various languages that are spoken today. Not only was the languages broken up, but God now scattered them all over the world. A fitting but mild end to a bad worship service experience.

Genesis 11:0-9

1 And the whole earth was of one language, and of one speech.

2 And it came to pass, as they journeyed from the east, that they found a plain in the land of Shinar; and they dwelt there.

3 And they said one to another, Go to, let us make brick, and burn them throughly. And they had brick for stone, and slime had they for morter.

4 And they said, Go to, let us build us a city and a tower, whose top may reach unto heaven; and let us make us a name, lest we be scattered abroad upon the face of the whole earth.

5 And the Lord came down to see the city and the tower, which the children of men builded.

6 And the Lord said, Behold, the people is one, and they have all one language; and this they begin to do: and now nothing will be restrained from them, which they have imagined to do.

7 Go to, let us go down, and there confound their language, that they may not understand one another's speech.

8 So the Lord scattered them abroad from thence upon the face of all the earth: and they left off to build the city.

9 Therefore is the name of it called Babel; because the Lord did there confound the language of all the earth: and from thence did the Lord scatter them abroad upon the face of all the earth.

Results = Babel = confusion, scattering.

God did not execute His severest judgement of killing and destruction upon them here, but only confused their speech and scattered the whole congregation of rebels across the earth. Babylon worship went with them as they were scattered all over the world.

BABYLON 2
Sodom and Gomorrah.
Sodom = a Canaanite city = Burning.
Gomorrah = Submersion.

Un-natural, perverted, confused, detestable abominable sexual conduct before a Holy God = a very grievous sin for which He utterly wastes and destroys, yes it's called Babylon worship.

God's fury and wrath was now on display here as the judgement against the twin cities of the ABOMINATION OF DESOLATION was destined for utter wasting and destruction. Sodomy, lesbianism, worshipping the heavenly bodies and child sacrifice goes hand in hand in Babylonian worship.

Genesis 18:20-23

20 And the Lord said, Because the cry of Sodom and Gomorrah is great, and because their sin is very grievous;
21 I will go down now, and see whether they have done altogether according to the cry of it, which is come unto me; and if not, I will know.
22 And the men turned their faces from thence, and went toward Sodom: but Abraham stood yet before the Lord.
23 And Abraham drew near, and said, Wilt thou also destroy the righteous with the wicked?

32 And he said, Oh let not the Lord be angry, and I will speak yet but this once: Peradventure ten shall be found there. And he said, I will not destroy it for ten's sake. 33 And the Lord went his way, as soon as he had left communing with Abraham: and Abraham returned unto his place.

***For the sake of ten righteous, God will spare a wicked city until He sees fit. Babylon's wickedness was on open display here, threats and intimidation of rape-sodomy by old and young men as they encircled Lot's house with his two male visitors like bees from every quarter.

Genesis 19:4-9

4 But before they lay down, the men of the city, even the men of Sodom, compassed the house round, both old and young, all the people from every quarter:
5 And they called unto Lot, and said unto him, Where are the men which came in to thee this night? bring them out unto us, that we may know them.
6 And Lot went out at the door unto them, and shut the door after him,
7 And said, I pray you, brethren, do not so wickedly.
8 Behold now, I have two daughters which have not known man; let me, I pray you, bring them out unto you, and do ye to them as is good in your eyes: only unto these men do nothing; for therefore came they under the shadow of my roof.
9 And they said, Stand back. And they said again, This one fellow came in to sojourn, and he will needs be a judge: now will we deal worse with thee, than with

them. And they pressed sore upon the man, even Lot, and came near to break the door.

***Even when offered two young virgin girls to satisfy their lust and pleasure, the men of Sodom flatly rejected the virgin girls, their desire was for the two strange men only who came into town that day and lodged in Lot's house, if they did not get the men, Lot was threatened that he himself would be the one raped, sodomized.

God pulls His righteous seed out of Babylon Sodom before it's total destruction.

Unknown to Lot and family, these two men were God's angels sent to rescue Him and family, and the angels lead them out of Sodom before the city's destruction.

Gen. 19 God's Word Translation.

12Then the men asked Lot, "Do you have anyone else here-any in-laws, sons, daughters, or any other relatives in the city? Get them out of here **13**because we're going to destroy this place. The complaints to the LORD against its people are so loud that the LORD has sent us to destroy it." **14**So Lot went out and spoke to the men engaged to his daughters.

He said, "Hurry! Get out of this place, because the LORD is going to destroy the city." But they thought he was joking and laughed at him.

***Upon publication of this book many may believe that I am joking also, just like Lot seemed to be joking, but The Lord has revealed all in this book to me.

So Sodom and Gomorrah was utterly wasted, destroyed by God. Not one lived, all died in that city.

Babylon Egypt 3

Egypt was utterly destroyed by God as shown in these scriptures. A Babylon type Empire that refused to heed God's warning to let His people go. Child sacrifices, false gods worshipped by the Egyptians (41 gods of Egypt) was a common practice. Egypt an Empire was allowed by God to grow and even blessed by God. He spared Egypt from a horrible famine in the days of Joseph His servant, because it fulfilled His purposes and plans for His people to survive and thrive, even in the midst of the ten plagues of Egypt.

Exodus 10 vs. 7

Pharaoh's servants said to him, "How long will this man be a snare to us? Let the men go, that they may serve the LORD their God. Do you not realize that Egypt is destroyed?"

Destruction of Egypt, even unknown to the madman Pharaoh, it was shattered as per this official's declaration. Pharaoh army was later destroyed in the Red Sea by The Lord closing it upon them.

Exodus 12

35The Israelites did what Moses had told them and asked the Egyptians for gold and silver jewelry and for clothes. 36The LORD made the Egyptians generous to the people, and they gave them what they asked for. So the Israelites stripped Egypt of its wealth

Upon the time appointed to leave Egypt by God, He made His people come out with great wealth, not dirt poor like they were all their lives in bondage, slavery.

Exodus 14

> .5When Pharaoh (the king of Egypt) was told that the people had fled, he and his officials changed their minds about them. They said, "What have we done? We've lost our slaves because we've let Israel go." 6So Pharaoh prepared his chariot and took his army with him. 7He took 600 of his best chariots as well as all the other chariots in Egypt, placing an officer in each of them.

Fool, rich, Pharaoh desires to rule over the poor always and keep them as slaves, but God has another agenda, shatter their chains of satanic rulership so His people can serve Him in freedom.

Babylon 4
Jericho = fragrant.

Jericho a pleasant fragrant place was turned into a stench of sinful wicked licentious worship before God, and God utterly destroyed it by fire through Joshua and his army in a miraculous rout.

Joshua 1:0-9

> 1 Now after the death of Moses the servant of the Lord it came to pass, that the Lord spake unto Joshua the son of Nun, Moses' minister, saying,
> 2 Moses my servant is dead; now therefore arise, go over this Jordan, thou, and all this people, unto the land which I do give to them, even to the children of Israel.

3 Every place that the sole of your foot shall tread upon, that have I given unto you, as I said unto Moses.

4 From the wilderness and this Lebanon even unto the great river, the river Euphrates, all the land of the Hittites, and unto the great sea toward the going down of the sun, shall be your coast.

5 There shall not any man be able to stand before thee all the days of thy life: as I was with Moses, so I will be with thee: I will not fail thee, nor forsake thee.

6 Be strong and of a good courage: for unto this people shalt thou divide for an inheritance the land, which I sware unto their fathers to give them.

7 Only be thou strong and very courageous, that thou mayest observe to do according to all the law, which Moses my servant commanded thee: turn not from it to the right hand or to the left, that thou mayest prosper whithersoever thou goest.

8 This book of the law shall not depart out of thy mouth; but thou shalt meditate therein day and night, that thou mayest observe to do according to all that is written therein: for then thou shalt make thy way prosperous, and then thou shalt have good success.

9 Have not I commanded thee? Be strong and of a good courage; be not afraid, neither be thou dismayed: for the Lord thy God is with thee whithersoever thou goest.

***God watered Joshua's spirit with these Words, a full discourse of instruction and encouragement in preparation to destroy a massive Babylon superpower fortresslike nation with massive security apparatus called Jericho. Jericho was a very great city with a massive amount of people in comparison to

Joshua and his army. But God does not deliver by might or numbers of men but by His Spirit alone.

The bigger they are and the harder they come, the harder they will all fall. When this biblical Babylon (Jericho) was encountered by Joshua, God charged Joshua and commanded him to be strong and very courageous, take down and destroy Jericho, burn it, and God gave Joshua a powerful strategy of how to get this job done, not by military strategies of men, but by God's BIBLE CODE 7 strategy. All God's victories boil down to one thing, a God given winning strategy. No strategy equals defeat, failure, wasting of time.

Joshua 6:3-5

3 And ye shall compass the city, all ye men of war, and go round about the city once. Thus shalt thou do six days.

4 And seven priests shall bear before the ark seven trumpets of rams' horns: and the seventh day ye shall compass the city seven times, and the priests shall blow with the trumpets.

5 And it shall come to pass, that when they make a long blast with the ram's horn, and when ye hear the sound of the trumpet, all the people shall shout with a great shout; and the wall of the city shall fall down flat, and the people shall ascend up every man straight before him.

***How is it known that this massive fortified Jericho was Babylon? Here's the answer without a doubt;

Joshua 7:20-21

20 And Achan answered Joshua, and said, Indeed I have sinned against the Lord God of Israel, and thus and thus have I done:

21 When I saw among the spoils a goodly Babylonish garment, and two hundred shekels of silver, and a wedge of gold of fifty shekels weight, then I coveted them, and took them; and, behold, they are hid in the earth in the midst of my tent, and the silver under it.

***The giveaway, a **Babylonish garment stolen by Achan**, symbolizing the culture and worship of these people of Jericho, that they were practitioners of Babylon worship, just like in the plains of Shinar at the Tower of Babel under Nimrod.

Babylon worship's penalty was meted out by a Holy Righteous God, total destruction of all people, young and old, animals, everything living must be killed as they were all an abomination to God, except the gold, silver, brass and iron must be brought out for the house of God. A powerful precedent is now set by God against all Babylon type empires, nations and worshippers.

Sodomy, pedophilia, incest, child human sacrifices, blood drinking was and is prevalent in all Babylon type worship activities as perversion from satan rules in this type of nation and worship services. Satan the liar, deceiver, perverter and corrupter, can never create, just pervert and corrupt that which God has made to be natural and healthy. Satan always goes against nature and what's natural like sodomy.

God's blood covered seed pulled out of Jericho–Babylon before it's total destruction.
Joshua 2

Good News Translation

24This is what you must do. When we invade your land, tie this red cord to the window you let us down from. Get your father and mother, your brothers, and all your father's family together in your house.

Joshua 6:25

25 And Joshua saved Rahab the harlot alive, and her father's household, and all that she had; and she dwelleth in Israel even unto this day; because she hid the messengers, which Joshua sent to spy out Jericho.

God warns His people do not get involved in Canaanite-Babylon worship, or else.
Lev. 18

20 Don't have sex with another man's wife—that would make you unclean.

21 Don't sacrifice your children on the altar fires to the god Molech. I am the LORD your God, and that would disgrace me.

22 It is disgusting for a man to have sex with another man.

23 Anyone who has sex with an animal is unclean.

24Don't make yourselves unclean by any of these disgusting practices of those nations that I am forcing out of the land for you. They made themselves 25and the land so unclean, that I punished the land because of their sins, and I made it vomit them up. 26-27Now don't do these sickening things that make the land filthy. Instead, obey my laws and teachings. 28Then the land won't become sick of you and vomit you up, just as it did them. 29-30If any of you do these vulgar, disgusting things, you will be unclean and no longer belong to my people. I am the LORD your God, and I forbid you to follow their sickening way of life.

BABYLON 5
The chosen Empire of God.

Daniel 4:9-18

9 O Belteshazzar, master of the magicians, because I know that the spirit of the holy gods is in thee, and no secret troubleth thee, tell me the visions of my dream that I have seen, and the interpretation thereof.

10 Thus were the visions of mine head in my bed; I saw, and behold a tree in the midst of the earth, and the height thereof was great.

11 The tree grew, and was strong, and the height thereof reached unto heaven, and the sight thereof to the end of all the earth:

12 The leaves thereof were fair, and the fruit thereof much, and in it was meat for all: the beasts of the field had shadow under it, and the fowls of the heaven dwelt in the boughs thereof, and all flesh was fed of it.

13 I saw in the visions of my head upon my bed, and, behold, a watcher and an holy one came down from heaven;

***The watcher angels of God oversees all things and all affairs of men on the whole earth and reports back to God.

14 He cried aloud, and said thus, Hew down the tree, and cut off his branches, shake off his leaves, and scatter his fruit: let the beasts get away from under it, and the fowls from his branches:

15 Nevertheless leave the stump of his roots in the earth, even with a band of iron and brass, in the tender grass of the field; and let it be wet with the dew of heaven, and let his portion be with the beasts in the grass of the earth:

16 Let his heart be changed from man's, and let a beast's heart be given unto him; and let seven times pass over him.

***Pride is a provocation that leads to God's destruction, What God has done before, if he did it then he can do it again.

17 This matter is by the decree of the watchers, and the demand by the word of the holy ones: to the intent that the living may know that the most High ruleth in the kingdom of men, and giveth it to whomsoever he will, and setteth up over it the basest of men.

***He rules over all things and in all men's affairs.

18 This dream I king Nebuchadnezzar have seen. Now thou, O Belteshazzar, declare the interpretation thereof, forasmuch as all the wise men of my kingdom are not able to make known unto me the interpretation: but thou art able; for the spirit of the holy gods is in thee.

***King Nebuchadnezzar sternly warned of not allowing his pride to consume him for it will surely destroy him. He was neither righteous nor merciful and was further warned about this deficit of his character.

Daniel 4:27-37

27 Wherefore, O king, let my counsel be acceptable unto thee, and break off thy sins by righteousness, and thine iniquities by shewing mercy to the poor; if it may be a lengthening of thy tranquillity.

28 All this came upon the king Nebuchadnezzar.

29 At the end of twelve months he walked in the palace of the kingdom of Babylon.

30 The king spake, and said, Is not this great Babylon, that I have built for the house of the kingdom by the might of my power, and for the honour of my majesty?

31 While the word was in the king's mouth, there fell a voice from heaven, saying, O king Nebuchadnezzar, to thee it is spoken; The kingdom is departed from thee.

32 And they shall drive thee from men, and thy dwelling shall be with the beasts of the field: they shall make thee to eat grass as oxen, and seven times shall pass over thee, until thou know that the most High ruleth in the kingdom of men, and giveth it to whomsoever he will.

33 The same hour was the thing fulfilled upon Nebuchadnezzar: and he was driven from men, and did eat grass as oxen, and his body was wet with the dew of heaven, till his hairs were grown like eagles' feathers, and his nails like birds' claws.

***The Lord struck him down immediately for his haughtiness and pride, instantly. Twelve months after he was warned about it, it happened, haughtiness and pride consumed him, he acted out of it and was instantly punished by the righteous judge.

King Nebuchadnezzar humbled, abased by God.

34 And at the end of the days I Nebuchadnezzar lifted up mine eyes unto heaven, and mine understanding returned unto me, and I blessed the most High, and I praised and honoured him that liveth for ever, whose dominion is an everlasting dominion, and his kingdom is from generation to generation:

35 And all the inhabitants of the earth are reputed as nothing: and he doeth according to his will in the army of heaven, and among the inhabitants of the earth: and none can stay his hand, or say unto him, What doest thou?

36 At the same time my reason returned unto me; and for the glory of my kingdom, mine honour and brightness returned unto me; and my counsellors and my lords sought unto me; and I was established in my kingdom, and excellent majesty was added unto me.

37 Now I Nebuchadnezzar praise and extol and honour the King of heaven, all whose works are truth, and his ways judgment: and those that walk in pride he is able to abase.

*** God now given the glory after this outburst of pride and punishment.

Destruction of Babylon 5

Babylon was as the scripture reveals here given massive dominion authority over vast regions of the earth and it's people by God. This was to rule over them and bring them into the knowledge of God. This was accomplished through king Nebuchadnezzar, now his son Belshazzar is king, and did not follow in his father's footsteps, how soon they forget, or do not desire to learn from the older generation. Belshazzar now grows up rebellious, proud and fun loving. Belshazzar now makes the same mistake as a king just as his father before him, but now worse in that he desecrated the Holy vessels of God in a drunken orgy with his pals. The response, the fury of God, God destroyed, gave a response immediately to his rebellion against him, the kingdom was overturned that very night. God hates pride and haughtiness;

Daniel 5:18-31

18 O thou king, the most high God gave Nebuchadnezzar thy father a kingdom, and majesty, and glory, and honour:
19 And for the majesty that he gave him, all people, nations, and languages, trembled and feared before him: whom he would he slew; and whom he would he kept alive; and whom he would he set up; and whom he would he put down.
20 But when his heart was lifted up, and his mind hardened in pride, he was deposed from his kingly throne, and they took his glory from him:

***Haughtiness and pride are the destroyers of men and Nations.

21 And he was driven from the sons of men; and his heart was made like the beasts, and his dwelling was with the wild asses: they fed him with grass like oxen, and his body was wet with the dew of heaven; till he knew that the most high God ruled in the kingdom of men, and that he appointeth over it whomsoever he will.

***God punishes swiftly the proud and arrogant.

22 And thou his son, O Belshazzar, hast not humbled thine heart, though thou knewest all this;

***Even though you knew this, you did not humble yourself, knowing but not doing what you know.

23 But hast lifted up thyself against the Lord of heaven; and they have brought the vessels of his house before thee, and thou, and thy lords, thy wives, and thy concubines, have drunk wine in them; and thou hast praised the gods of silver, and gold, of brass, iron, wood, and stone, which see not, nor hear, nor know: and the God in whose hand thy breath is, and whose are all thy ways, hast thou not glorified:

***Belshazzar's pride rose up in him and caused him to do an evil thing, lift up himself against God Himself. Fools rise up against God because they say in their hearts there is no God.

God's Holy vessels and Words were desecrated, mocked, ridiculed and glory given to another god, the fury of God now rose up and consumed them. God's judgement follows hard on the heels of desecration of His name and Word through haughtiness and pride.

24 Then was the part of the hand sent from him; and this writing was written.

25 And this is the writing that was written, MENE, MENE, TEKEL, UPHARSIN.

26 This is the interpretation of the thing: MENE; God hath numbered thy kingdom, and finished it.

27 TEKEL; Thou art weighed in the balances, and art found wanting.

28 PERES; Thy kingdom is divided, and given to the Medes and Persians.

***This is where the statement, **"the handwriting or warning is on the wall"** is taken from.

Babylon 5 was now handed over to the Medes and the Persians (modern day Iran) to be destroyed by them under General Darius that very same night.

29 Then commanded Belshazzar, and they clothed Daniel with scarlet, and put a chain of gold about his neck, and made a proclamation concerning him, that he should be the third ruler in the kingdom.

30 In that night was Belshazzar the king of the Chaldeans slain.

***That very night, Babylon 5 was wasted, utterly destroyed, suddenly. The peace and safety that was declared, we have the strongest military, nice fancy missiles and bombs, no one can defeat us, we are invincible, they bragged, boasted but The Lord raised up an adversary to work through and they were utterly, suddenly destroyed, fulfilling His Word;

31 And Darius the Median took the kingdom, being about threescore and two years old.

Proverbs 16:18
18 Pride goeth before destruction, and an haughty spirit before a fall.

BABYLON 6
Babylon USA's coming destruction revealed.
The great EMIGRATION from the USA.

The Christian life is one of going upstream in a down-stream world.

The destruction of Babylon USA began when the prayers were removed from the schools by the Supreme Court on the ruling of the lawsuit brought by Madalyn Murray O'hare in 1962. At that point the dragon, satan invaded the USA, it's Schools, Universities and it's society. The USA then began it's rapid deep descent into the abyss of demoralization and confusion, as it's people were profiled and indoctrinated to respond in a certain preconceived manner, no God.

Enter the dragon once more when the hippie movement emerged and the entertainment scene was overtaken and dominated by Chinese Kung Fu Fighting movies. This was the satanic one two punch, the anti Jesus Synagogue of satan crowd, who are in spiritual bondage to satan will go berserk and seek to chastise and castigate, but we are untouchable to them by the release of His Word, which is a minesweeper over our lives through BIBLE CODE 7.

In the same manner as Lot was looked at by his sons in law to be out of his mind crazy, is in the same manner many will believe that the weaponization of God's Word is crazy.

But who won and who lost? Lot won as the Angel of God led him out of Sodom he, his wife and daughters. However, Mrs. Lot's heart stayed in Sodom, she was a sodomite sympathizer and was turned into a pillar of salt as she did not really desire to leave Sodom.

It is in this same manner that many will perish because of what I reveal in this book regarding the USA from God's Word. The USA is headed down a turbocharged path to destruction, riding a tsunami of abominations, wickedness and immoralities.

God's people should be warned to vacate it in a timely manner because of what will soon happen, it's total takedown and destruction is coming just as God spelt it out in this His Word that I reveal. Christianity and conservatism, the keeping of the old beliefs of faith in Christianity and clinging to the old values thereof (This could be wrapped up in the ten commandments) is losing the youth of America and the world, to liberalism and secularism which throws off inhibitions and restraints, the checks and balances that keeps a society in moral balance;

Psalm 2

2Kings take their stands. Rulers make plans together against the LORD and against his Messiah by saying, 3"Let's break apart their chains and shake off their ropes."

America in these modern times has digressed to follow and practice old Babylon religion and worship with it's child sacrifices to Merodach or Moloch. Approximately sixty five million babies have been aborted in USA since Roe vs. Wade verdict, and in June of 2016, sodomy and lesbianism was also made legal by the aristocratic demonic Supreme Court USA ruling against The Lord, and in favor of the demonic overlords. Cannibalism, human and baby blood sacrifices are prevalent and increasing in the USA rapidly so as to gain power with satan. The USA has cast Jesus Christ aside and has invited and embraced many false religions and gods in His place. Just recently the Supreme Court has sided in a ruling with the State of Nevada that forces the Churches to conform to the laws of men and restricts their freedom of worship, 50 persons maximum capacity at one time even if they have a 1,000 seat sanctuary, treating the Churches less than other businesses, and stipulating the Churches are non essential unlike other businesses in that State, that can have gathered at one time, 50% of their fire code capacity.

The beginning of Babylon five's empire was in Iraq/Iran which is the kingdom of Persia. It's interesting to note that the Bushes, Presidents 1 and 2 both attacked this area, once each. This area, I believe, is integral to the new world order and the maintenance of Babylon USA. Both Bushes were new world order globalists. This is the reason why the USA has military bases firmly entrenched there in Iraq along with 800 military bases all over the world in over 70 nations. I also believe that these bases are not just military bases, but a spiritual outpost to attempt constraining the Prince of Persia, that territorial demon, and to converse with him regarding rulership of the whole world in the new one world Babylon order.

The new One World Order, Novus Ordo Seclorum, seen on the USA dollar bill, was entered into at Babylon- Shinar, reinforced at Babylon Iraq, and then Babylon USA for this New World Order to take root and grow. This system however, will never override or overrule the New World Order System in the Blood Covenant of Jesus Christ, and must be destroyed, for of His Kingdom, there shall be no end.

Babylon system = satanic world system.

The nomenclature used at the invasion of Iraq was **"Shock n awe"**, could it also be a reference to the word **"Shekinah"** as a deep spiritual connection to Iraq, Babylon 5 has been demonstrated by the Presidents Bushes in two separate attacks on this nation?

The occult layout of Washington D.C., especially around the White House and the Washington Monuments can be seen by the naked eye, hidden in plain sight, and there is an occult, dark hidden connection between USA and Babylon Iraq.

A few US Administrations ago, then current President George W. Bush shocked the whole USA and the world when he announced that he was a Skull and Bones secret society member, so secret was this society that he could say no more. As a **bonesman**, a secret society that does not pray to Jesus Christ, but worships satan, we know that this was a demonic society entrenched at the top levels of the U.S. Government with a President now in office.

Justice Felix Frankfurter once said,"Real rulers in Washington D.C. are invisible and exercise power from behind the scenes."

Take another careful look at the USA's one dollar bill and see below the pyramid the words, "NOVUS ORDO SECLORUM", meaning- New Order of the Ages" This is coded language that the sons of darkness will arise one day to battle the sons of light, the sons of God in a duel and there will be a struggle which they anticipate winning. Please understand very carefully that demons go where they are invited, just like Jesus and His Holy Angels, and the demons have been invited by the USA's founders and leaders past and present to come here, stay here and lead this nation in their direction. Evil demons have been enthroned in Washington D.C. to stay and guide this nation in satan's will and way since it's founding in July 4th, 1776.

This is symbolized on the dollar bill, the USA's calling card, by the top pyramid, the enlightened ones, above the bottom pyramid, representing the masses of uninformed gullible people in the USA, and showing their domination and rulership over them. The more things change, the more it stays the same. Have you ever noticed that whatever political party is in power in the USA, their policies are the same? Seems like they both are one party, two sides of the same coin, an illusion and great deception of the people of the USA into believing that they are different. It is all controlled from behind the scenes by powerful men to direct the path of this nation and by even more powerful men in the world to direct the path of the whole world into a one world rulership, religion and currency.

Be not deceived, the back of the Good Book says so.

What do we the Church do?

Rise up in rebellion, in strength not weakness, and begin to condemn, denounce, prophesy against evil leaders worldwide. Pray for those destined for salvation that they will come quickly to embrace Jesus, and lastly, to make a move to get out of the USA and go back to your own land as the Word reveals and the Holy Spirit leads you.

All it needs for evil to proliferate is for good men and women, Christians to do nothing, not knowing that they have the greatest power here on earth at their disposal, the Word of God in prayer warfare, BIBLE CODE 7.

So let's weaponize the Word of God, the sword of the Spirit by which we fight. Our life preservation and self defense strategy, BIBLE CODE 7. The era of great tribulation along with it's massive deception has been ushered in, fallen upon the whole world where the whole world is being deceived all at once, en masse through the medium of the internet and it's various components. News travel incredibly swift and just as Goebbels, Adolph Hitler's Minister of Propaganda said, "If you tell a lie, big enough, long enough, and loud enough, people will believe it." So powerful and so true. This is satan's prime method of operation, lies and deceits as satan is the father and originator of all lies from the beginning.

There are many old and evil roots to be dealt with in America

True reality is that America's social order has never been entirely equitable. While we're not using police to manage slavery as the police used to do at their inception of colonialism today, we are using police to manage the problems that this very unequal system has produced which is;

***A spiritual multi generational curse upon the slave descendants and the slave owners descendants. This is a spiritual problem which cannot be addressed by physical means. To fully address this problem at the root, There must be an emancipation from demonic spiritual slavery, bondage. The slave descendants police and slave owners that are operating and acting from under this curse. They are acting out from under the oppression of demons. This I addressed in detail in my book "Escaping the Ultimate Deception- Counterfeit through BIBLE CODE 7."

The history of law enforcement which started out in the days of slavery to track down and return runaway slaves, results in black people being killed by police at a disproportionate rate, advocates say. A paper in 2016 in the American Journal of Preventive Medicine analyzed data from the National Violent Death Reporting System, a federally maintained database. It found that although the majority of victims of lethal force by police were white, the **fatality rate** among black people was 2.8 times higher than among white people. Here is some evidence that the generational demon of the slave enforcers are at work very actively in todays culture, demons do not die, just go from one generation to the next, different days same things.

So without going to the very root of the problem, the multigenerational curse of colonialism slavery, all we are doing is delaying the inevitable, applying a bandaid, because the problem is (1) recognizing that there is a spiritual dimension to these conditions, (2) That the SYSTEM is corrupt, the system is RIGGED against the slave descendants and in favor of the slave owners, the ruling class wealthy elites that rules over the world.

"The rich rules over the poor, borrowers are slaves to the lenders."

The world's systems are rigged and rigged against the masses and in favor of the ruling class upper crust.

Allow me to introduce a new word in the cultural vocabulary. This word is **"THE TEN PERCENTERS"**

What does this mean?

This is the name God has revealed to me about a hidden select group of people that has been copied from the Bible, these belong to satan and satan calls them his children. I used to follow the reading and claim of the wealthy One percenters, who control 50-55 % of the world's wealth. The Lord spoke to me and said that as I looked at the pyramid on the money, a one dollar bill, the pyramid has a base and so does the one percenters need a base to rest on, to spread out their misery and power, so they are coupled with nine percent more to become TEN PERCENT.

From Tele Sur English.net Nov 22, 2016

The Richest 10 Percent Control 89 Percent of the World's Wealth.

CNBC 85% world's wealth controlled by 10%

10% of the world controls 85 % of the world's wealth, leaving 90% of the world to fight for a meager 15 % of the world's wealth, Do you understand this? Satan imitates Jesus always, the tithe belongs to the Lord, 10% of all earnings, so does 10% of all people belong to the Lord, those who will love and serve Him. Straight and narrow is the way to heaven and few find it, 10%. Versus broad is the way to hell an many go into it, 90%.

Jesus encountered a group of ten lepers, of which all were healed through His common grace to all mankind. Only one returned to worship and thank Him. So Jesus asked that one leper this powerfully revealing question;

Luke 17:15-18

15 And one of them, when he saw that he was healed, turned back, and with a loud voice glorified God,
16 And fell down on his face at his feet, giving him thanks: and he was a Samaritan.
17 And Jesus answering said, Were there not ten cleansed? but where are the nine?
18 There are not found that returned to give glory to God, save this stranger.

The one out of ten, or **Jesus's TEN PERCENT salvation message**. The common grace of God is given to all ten people, however none will return to freely lovingly worship and serve Him except one, or TEN PERCENT, one out of ten. This ten percent symbolizes the tithe that belongs to God almighty and must be given to Him alone and always.

This is the revelation of the Lord's TEN PERCENTERS to me.

So satan follows suit and gives his children 10% of the world's population, control and ownership of 85% of the world's wealth. Thus the name

SATAN"S TEN PERCENTERS.

Caution: not all wealthy belong to satan, God has many in the ten percent wealthiest group, Just like Joseph of Arithamea.

2 rigged systems govern the entire world.
System #1

System of man, Globalism Babylon, which is under satan's control.

The USA is on trial in front of the whole world as it's leadership and promotion of freedom and democracy is under vicious attack, but the cracks and fissures of it's system being rigged is wide open for all the world to see. It has been and still is rigged against the Indians, African American minority, against other minority people, the masses, and in favor of the celebrity justice rich and famous, oligarchs ruling class.

This rigging is deeper than the eyes can see and brains can be wrapped around. At the root of the matter, is the USA under President Trump's leadership which is anti Globalist or anti new world order vs. globalism, new world order, even some well positioned influential wealthy people in the USA who are fighting viciously against him and his policies. They want him out of office, period, so a new globalist minded President can be positioned there. President Trump is a Patriot, not a globalist which is great. One of the first moves he made upon becoming President was to remove the USA from the Paris Climate Agreement of 2015. This agreement was a lead up to Agenda 2021, and this is the crux of the matter, globalism is rejected by Trump and most of the informed, sound thinking American people who have a brain to think with. The globalists are fighting to have him removed from office at any cost and by any means possible. The new world order crowd and agenda has been stalled for now by Mr Trump being President, but not destroyed, as their proponents are still viciously fighting to remove him by any means, even revolutionary violence.

The system is rigged in favor of the Ten Percenters, the bankers of Basel, the Davos gang, rich oligarchs, royals, nobilities, ruling class and their enforcers-maintainers of their status quo, the courts, law making bodies from the highest to the lowest using the laws or men, law enforcement and the prisons. The whole system is rigged and infiltrated by secret society groups.

Law and order shouted out, is never about God's law and order, **the 10 commandments,** but men's law. It's called the beast system, and satan with his ten percenters controls this system, this is the root of all problems today.

At the root of this beast system is the love of money.

Laws, rules and regulations are made by and for the rich ruling class, to suit them by the law making bodies. The Book of Daniel teaches us that. A law, a legal decree was made for all people by the unscrupulous with a motive, and when that decree was broken, then, either bow to the system or burn, or be thrown in the Lion's den.

Get WOKE people. History is repeating itself as the BIBLE is never wrong, irrelevant, outdated or obsolete, but a relevant and pertinent document for cradle to grave powerful, successful dynamic living and for all times.

Today, apparent for all to see is, that Lady justice is peeking out from under her blindfold to see who is approaching her to receive justice. If you're not part of the system, the rich, secret society groups, sorry the scales of justice are weighed against you, you're not one of us, you don't serve us, we can't help you, you have no immunity. All those who serve our system, have immunity from the same laws that governs the masses. Rules for thee, but not for us. If you're one of us you're immune, if you're not one of us, you have no immunity, Lady justice says from behind her blindfold.

You have been weighed in the balances of Lady Justice's system and found lacking, you're not one of us, so no justice for you.

Open your eyes and see this is the crux of the matter, do not be deceived by being thrown a bone of appeasement, as you're not a dog.

The theory and practice of oligarchic, Ten Percenters, ruling class rulership is to make things much harder than they need to be for the people, the masses, so that when they cry out, any concession or any let up that is given, the ruling class begins to look so great, they are made to seem like heroes or deliverers and they try to make themselves look so good anyway and anyhow.

The key strategy of the rich, is to keep the masses of the people on the back foot, unbalanced, off guard, poor and miserable from cradle to grave.

Hosea 4-6,

6I will destroy my people because they are ignorant. You have refused to learn, so I will refuse to let you be my priests. You have forgotten the teachings of your God, so I will forget your children.

Once in a while the system might throw one of it's own, someone into the lion's den, under the bus to make a point, to make the system look good, but that's for show, window dressing, for behind the scenes they will be buttered up with a financial parachute, because they serve the beast system. It's an us against them rigged system.

Never forget...Prov. 22-7. The rich rules over the Poor... this status quo must not be broken but must be maintained at all costs by the ultra rich.

Never forget the ultra rich, Pharaoh class is ruling, that class says I will never let you go, you exist to serve me. There are round table conferences of planners for satan's Ten Percenters that constantly plot strategies under satan's leadership to keep the masses of people in bondage one of which is the World Economic Forum, the Davos gang and the bankers of Basel Switzerland.

Best example, look carefully at the U.S. Dollar bill. Look carefully at the top pyramid with the eye in it, that is the Ten Percenters vs. the bottom part of the pyramid representing the masses, do you get the message?

Never forget that, hidden hand secret societies dominate this system and world and make it seem untouchable, but it's not. Jesus can and will shatter it through His Word declared from your lips.

Do you know and understand the depth of the enemy to deceive? Did you know that the the devil even funds and starts churches, so he can try to deceive the very elect, God's people.

Satanic king Henry #8, started the rebel Church of England which is the national and official Church of England.

The immunity of the select, ruling class untouchables from their injustices and oppressions, the teflon few, with their celebrity justice is rubbed very often in the eyes of the angry fuming masses who fume but shut up and do nothing, thus the reason for writing this book, fume yes but do something, fight through BIBLE CODE 7 minesweeping warfare strategy.

All of this system serves the Rich, not only the Bible tells us that but the history books also, remember the French Revolution? It would behoove you to search the internet and do a quick read of it and it's ultimate outcome.

Zoophilia, bestiality Has become rampant in the USA, Babylon's society with it's perverted and corrupted sexual love for their beloved family pets.

Pedophilia. The most heinous crime, the abuse of the innocent little children by wicked men and women.

Child trafficking. The sexual exploitation of, and prostitution of the little boys and girls for money. The largest money making business in the USA. This shows the depravity of a nation and it's people.

Solution; BIBLE CODE 7.

Just like repellent spray to keep off mosquitoes, so is The WORD of God, this is your repellent spray from the abundance of your heart against all demonic dark forces.

System #2

The Jesus system is the eternally prevailing system, for of His kingdom there shall be no end. All those who love the Jesus system, shall be hanging out with Jesus now and for all eternity because we trust in Him and His system alone, His Word.

The USA, the sorcerer, evil magic nation is judged by God Almighty and sentenced to fail and fall. In little more than one hundred years, the USA went from a God fearing Jesus loving nation to a nation that rejected Him outright and showed the world it did so by it's calling card, the great seal of the USA placed upon it's prime currency the dollar bill in 1786.

The USA was chosen by satan and his agents long ago to spawn, give birth to the anti christ or son of perdition. This I will label as the AGENDA.

The role of sorcery- Pharmakeia in the USA's destruction.

Pharmakeia = occult magic, sorcery, witchcraft, drug abuse, misuse of drugs to poison not cure, legalized recreational drugs.

Sorcery (Strong's Concordance) = pharmakeia, administering of drugs, poisoning, sorcery, magical arts, the deceptions of idolatry.

I will exclude medicinal drugs from this as God is not against medicines, or a balm in Gilead, neither Physicians. Medicines have a totally different meaning as medicines are used for healing, a balm.

There is a drug for everything in the USA. These drugs are not only for medicinal purposes, but also recreational. Drugs are in most cases synthesized, patented, lab made produced in a laboratory, and not natural.

Medicinal drugs have been around and used for hundreds of years and referred to as medicines, but the word drugs later took on the meaning of a substance to open the gates to the occult world to bring one into an altered state of consciousness just like alcohol, pharmakeia. Many sorcerers have also joined in and concocted potions, lotions, brews to be used for occult reasons, rituals, to enhance, to make or compel one to do something under demonic spells associated with it, to hex or curse. Foods, beverages, all products sold in the open marketplaces, even in very luxurious offices can be bewitched, drugs added, to make people strongly desire to purchase them, or for them to become addictive, habit forming. When foods or beverages are consumed they taste really good because they just might be enhanced with a drug, a food enhancer to make people love and keep on buying and consuming it, this means more money for the manufacturers.

Drugs and alcohol are usually banded together as a group and go hand in hand. The USA has a get high culture and appetite that must be fed, these types of drugs that feed it are legal and illegal, both fuel a multi billion dollar drug industry.

Source (U.S. news.com) estimates that 146 Billion dollars worth of (get high) drugs were sold in the USA in 2016.

From the massive use of get high drugs, alcohol, occult potions, the combined results are dire, like insanity, addictions, crime, immoralities, the spread of diseases, newborn inherited diseases from mothers, eventually leading to death of the abusers. 'Those who practice these works of the flesh will not inherit the kingdom of God', even though they are legalized.

Medicinal drugs have veered off course sharply of late, things that are spiritual in nature are now being treated by physical (drugs) means, man made drugs. Inundated tv ads, multiple prescribed drugs for almost every ache, pain, or symptom fuels a massive drug industry. My opinion, many Doctors have now become pill pushers, and not truly medical Practitioners.

For the blatant use of sorceries, these are the prophecied ends of the USA;

Isaiah 47:9

9 But these two things shall come to thee in a moment in one day, the loss of children, and widowhood: they shall come upon thee in their perfection for the multitude of thy sorceries, and for the great abundance of thine enchantments.

***Simon the sorcerer used the same manipulative sorcery upon a geographical area named Samaria;

Acts 8:11

11 And to him they had regard, because that of long time he had bewitched them with sorceries.

Revelation 9:21

21 Neither repented they of their murders, nor of their sorceries, nor of their fornication, nor of their thefts.

***To their utter destruction;

Revelation 18:23

23 And the light of a candle shall shine no more at all in thee; and the voice of the bridegroom and of the bride shall be heard no more at all in thee: for thy merchants were the great men of the earth; for by thy sorceries were all nations deceived

Chapter 2

Navigating the great tribulation times and season through BIBLE CODE 7.

Sanction and embargo satan and your adversaries with the Word of God.

Hello paycheck to paycheck'ers this is for you, first, get my book

"The Hundredfold through BIBLE CODE 7"

Make up your mind, "NO MORE CRUMBS", crumb days are over.

Jesus destined a hundredfold for you here in this world and in this life;

For you to be a part of the richer 50% of the world all you need is to have $4,300.00 to your name. If you don't, then you belong to the poorer 50% or poorer half of the world. Now for you to belong to the upper 10% of the world that owns and controls 85% of the world's wealth, all you need is a net worth of $93,170.00.

Need to be a one percenter? Then all needed is a net worth of $871,320.00 then you are now a one percenter, but make sure you're on **Jesus's side as not all ten or one percenters are evil.** Before Moses led God's people out of Egypt, they were given gold, silver, changes of clothes by the Egyptians, in like manner you will not leave Babylon USA empty handed;

Matthew 19:29

29 And every one that hath forsaken houses, or brethren, or sisters, or father, or mother, or wife, or children, or lands, for my name's sake, shall receive an hundredfold, and shall inherit everlasting life.

If you ever find yourself in a ship that is always leaking, the energy spent in jumping ship, will be much better spent than constantly patching it's leaks. The ship is un-salvageable, so says The Lord about Babylon USA.

The foundational pillars upon which the USA was founded and built have eroded, and are crumbling more before our very eyes. The USA is not salvageable and there is no turning back, no healing for the USA because God has already made up His mind about it's destruction, His Word declares several times from several prophets the destruction that He is going to bring upon it. The stench of this nation's sin has reached into His nostrils and He is ballistically angry, (wroth) with this nation and it's wicked rulers. There might be some delays in judgement because of the cry of His children that are still here, but the judgement is sure to come. The collapse of the USA is unavoidable and inevitable, but can however be delayed by the prayers and repentance of the saints, just like Nineveh, but never denied. Judgement delayed is never judgement denied, as desecration must always lead to judgement. There will be no patching of the leaks on Titanic USA, it will surely crash and sink as the mind of The Lord has determined it, and the mouth of The Lord has spoken it sternly. All that is left of the House USA is a few pieces of it's great foundation like the love of freedom and the yearning for individual expression. The evil ten percenters ruling class overlords have wrecked this nation and steered it into satan's den since it's very birth.

The Days of Herod are here.

The handwriting is on the wall, the warning to all Christians that the time is at hand, the beginning of the persecution of the Christian Churches has now begun, and any watchman on the wall of Christian fasting and prayers should see that this has now begun to happen.

The Church of Jesus Christ is now being persecuted under the pretext of Covid 19 which is a diabolically hatched scheme. Churches are being mandated to have no more than fifty persons in their worship services, even if their capacity is 2-5,000 people. The mandate is that the peoples temperature must be taken and a sign in sheet must be kept. Social distancing must be practiced and of course mask wearing and no singing or chanting. Under this mandate there must be no baptism or laying on of hands, neither hugging. The rules for the Churches are now more strict than that of going into a major store to make purchases. The resulting conditions are that one third of the Church members surveyed said they will not go back to Church for worship services, (Barna Research) and many weak Christians who were weak to begin with will fall away from or desert the faith. It's a well thought out plot as the Churches have been labelled non-essential businesses and forced to close along with restaurants, bars, and gyms. There are reports now coming in that many Church buildings are being set on fire, the works of arsonists. With one stroke satan's globalist agents in Government have wreaked havoc in the Churches and have caused them to shut down and many will never reopen, but go bankrupt, tithes and offerings are diminished or non existent as many members reason, If I don't go to church I don't need to give the tithe. The Churches are now going back to the future where it first began, in homes with small groups. The Church should never wait to be attacked, there is a response to be given always by the diligent awoke Church that's always on the offensive, it's biblical, in the Bible and should always be followed, here it is:

Weakness begs aggression. A warning to the Christian saints. The only fear of the satanists globalists–the Word of God from your lips.
Acts 12 GNT Translation
> 1About this time King Herod+ began to persecute some members of the church. 2He had James, the brother of John, put to death by the sword.

***James butchered for being a Christian, his head chopped off. The result the lazy, sleeping, foolish Christians did nothing, a pile of rubbish, teddy bears, flowers and candles were left at a spot for James as a memorial.

> 3When he saw that this pleased the Jews, he went ahead and had Peter arrested. (This happened during the time of the Festival of Unleavened Bread.)

***Peter was now ambushed and set up to be butchered after Easter, because the lazy sleeping Church did nothing regarding James. Weakness begs for aggression.

A blood lust rests upon the Jews from of the days Saul killed the Gibeonites. God referred to this as the bloody house of Saul. Here is where that blood lust comes from here;

2 Samuel 21:1

1 Then there was a famine in the days of David three years, year after year; and David enquired of the Lord. And the Lord answered, It is for Saul, and for his bloody house, because he slew the Gibeonites.

***This blood lust came down the spiritual generational lines and is seen demonstrated here in plain sight. Only Jesus Christ's blood can wash away the sinful wicked nature of men.

4 After his arrest Peter was put in jail, where he was handed over to be guarded by four groups of four soldiers each. Herod planned to put him on trial in public after Passover. 5 So Peter was kept in jail, but the people of the church were praying earnestly to God for him.

***The lazy foolish Christians did nothing when James was killed, so they'll kill again, their enemy sees them as sheep to be slaughtered so let's do it again with one of their leaders, they say. This Church has James's blood on their hands as they did absolutely nothing.

Now the true Church, the sleeping giant got woke and began to do what the true Church should always do without waiting for a crisis to happen so they can respond, by '**praying without ceasing', this is what they should have done in the first place, and kept on doing. Being always on the offensive,**

never defensive. A no idle angels policy! Striking the enemy with fire and fury.

This is the true business of the true Church, and if the Church is not doing this then close the doors.

Peter Is Set Free from Prison.

6The night before Herod was going to bring him out to the people, Peter was sleeping between two guards. He was tied with two chains, and there were guards on duty at the prison gate. 7Suddenly an angel of the Lord stood there, and a light shone in the cell. The angel shook Peter by the shoulder, woke him up, and said, "Hurry! Get up!" At once the chains fell off Peter's hands. 8Then the angel said, "Tighten your belt and put on your sandals." Peter did so, and the angel said, "Put your cloak around you and come with me."

***Without praying in this manner, the Church is wasting it's time. God cannot respond to a prayer less Church, and James died in vain because of a lazy irresponsible Church leadership and body.

Now the true Church awoke and arose and did what they should be doing from the start, God responded and did as He always wanted to do, **dispatch angels** to protect His precious saints, just as He swore He would do. Without calling unto God, to allow Him to answer and demonstrate His power to us, we tie His hands. So let's keep our angels busy working as they do not ever get tired, policy; NO IDLE ANGELS;

Psalm 91:10-12

10 There shall no evil befall thee, neither shall any plague come nigh thy dwelling.

11 For he shall give his angels charge over thee, to keep thee in all thy ways.

12 They shall bear thee up in their hands, lest thou dash thy foot against a stone.

***Let the Church now arise to power and prayer warfare, by using the spiritual nuclear option of God, declaring the Word of God only, in prayer through BIBLE CODE 7.

2 Timothy 1:7

7 For God hath not given us the spirit of fear; but of power, and of love, and of a sound mind.

Beware of Pastors preaching that we are our brothers keepers. Yes, we are our Christian sisters and brothers keepers, but never the keeper of all mankind. We are admonished by Jesus to be good to all men, showing love and human kindness to all men, however we are to go above and beyond, be especially good to the household of faith. There is a difference, I must love my Christian brothers and sisters, regardless of our differences, and I am to be their keepers, as they are my keepers. I am obligated by The Lord to go the extra mile for them, but never the keepers of the world outside the Church. There is no obligation to them. They will see and experience Jesus's love, kindness and generosity through me and give glory to my father in heaven, but my Christian brothers and sisters will experience Jesus's love, kindness, compassion, prayers, generosity in overflowing abundance, to the max through me. The blood of Jesus ties us together as one. Christians do not have to beg for a brother or sister to be their keepers, there is an abundance of them in the Churches of Jesus Christ, those that name the name of Jesus, aged and young, in foreign lands through missions, and those close by.

A quantum shift has occurred, and a new era has now begun in USA.
Sensitivity training, re education or indoctrination camps coming soon.

I am writing on this topic here as the reality of our customs, traditions and outlooks will have to be altered, changed because of the great tribulation era that we have entered and the death Agenda of the globalists implemented for sustainable development. A change has occurred, a shift made, the world has changed overnight as if it has shifted into high gear in three months since Covid began. God warned us in the Book of Jeremiah, that the period of running with the footmen in a footrace would be over, and the new era of running with horsemen would begin. A time of great wickedness and great evil turned loose upon the people by the satanic globalists which would usher in the swelling of Jordan. This Word of God is evident and clear and the best explainer of what's happening now;

Jeremiah 12. Contemporary English Version
Jeremiah Complains to the LORD

1Whenever I complain
to you, LORD,
you are always fair.
But now I have questions
about your justice.
Why is life easy for sinners?
Why are they successful?
2You plant them like trees;
you let them prosper

and produce fruit.
Yet even when they praise you,
they don't mean it.

3But you know, LORD,
how faithful I've always been,
even in my thoughts.
So drag my enemies away
and butcher them like sheep!

4How long will the ground be dry
and the pasturelands parched?
The birds and animals
are dead and gone.
And all of this happened because
the people are so sinful.
They even brag, "God can't see
the sins we commit."+
The LORD Answers Jeremiah
5Jeremiah, if you get tired
in a race against people,
how can you possibly run
against horses?
If you fall in open fields,
what will happen in the forest
along the Jordan River?
6Even your own family
has turned against you.
They act friendly,
but don't trust them.
They're out to get you,
and so is everyone else.

This is a message from the Lord given to me to publish from His own mouth, His Word, to reveal to all who read this book and the whole world, a new era of great tribulation has now begun upon the face of the earth. The swelling of the Jordan has begun. The running with the horsemen has now begun. The only secure destination and hiding place is in Jesus Christ and the only strategy of warfare for this fight is BIBLE CODE 7, giving the battle to The Lord as it belongs to Him and not us. Re education and indoctrination camps are already here in China and coming to the USA, what will your answer be when told you need **sensitivity training, re education training, to keep your job? What will you be trained to be sensitive to, and what will you need to be re educated about?**

To re educate from your freedom and rugged individuality to total obedience of the rulers of the masses, obedience or die?

The actuality of sickness, death and dying must be revamped in the light of all we see going on today. The precious saints of God along with many who are not believers, who believe in the extending of their loved ones existence till a hundred years old, if possible, even if a chronic illness strikes and there is absolutely no quality of life left. We hold dearly to life and even fast and pray to preserve life for a loved one 80-100 years old, that they will live even longer even on a bed of total care need. Families who must pay out of pocket for doctors and medications must begin to think clearly about the entire scenario and make an assessment of whether to pray and ask God for His mercy in delivering the very aged and ill to take them home, if their souls are right with God.

I recount several years ago two sisters in the Lord that I know, and also a brother who was a Pastor who asked for prayers of cessation of life because they knew and were assured of a better place, Paradise, a need to end the pain and suffering and their need not to be an emotional and financial burden to their families. A reassessment of death and dying must be made.

Covid 19 deaths has been a wake up call as many funerals cannot be had or attended (Limited Attendees) except on social media or the internet for loved ones who have passed away. This evaluation must be made as to whether we pray and ask for God's mercy to end life on earth with it's pain and suffering or continue to ask God for life for which there is no quality, or to make it so that we be absent from the body, then present with the Lord. The average age of Covid 19 victims are 78 years old.

God given visions and revelations.
A second vision of gasoline shortages in the USA in the latter half of 2020

In this vision, my second vision with President Trump, I was called out of my vehicle by a secret service man and told, "the President needs to talk with you." I got out of my car, followed the man and went to a limousine where the President was seated facing the rear of the car. I got inside, but there was a man with his back turned to me sitting on the seat I sat on, I sat beside him facing the President. I do not remember the topic of conversation, however as we spoke , the President pressed the window button to put the window down. As he did this the man whose back was turned to me pressed the button to put the window up. There was now a tug of war between this man and the President pushing the button down and being resisted by the man pushing the window up. This went on for a while and it became apparent to me that the President was being resisted at every action, decision and the outcome makes it seem that he is not in control of the presidency, bumbling and foolish.

The opposite of what he wants done is being done, at every turn and action.

I left the meeting and went to a very close by gas station. I paid for the gas inside then went out and started to gas up the SUV I was driving. As I was gassing up, the gas stopped flowing from the nozzle. I was alarmed as I knew I had not reached the amount I paid for, then suddenly I heard someone cry out, "There's no gas, the gas has run out".

I then woke up out of this vision.

My third vision of a gasoline shortage in the USA. 7/10/2020

I was driving on a local road and needed gas. as I approached the gas station, I noticed a long line to get into the station, so I went past the station to enter from the opposite side. I was stunned, the line was just as long. Not only at that gas station but at other gas stations.

I know this is a prophetic vision to let me know that as the third vision seen, about a gas shortage in the USA, the world's largest oil producer will run out of gasoline at the pumps, it will surely happen. How and why? The Lord did not reveal that to me. But it will happen, there will be a terrible gas shortage at the pumps.

A vision of paying with a strange new currency 7/12/2020

I am not able to remember all details of this vision, but the dynamic portion of it was I saw and focused for a long time on a strange new currency in my hand. A currency I have never seen before. I had two of them that seemed like a 500 valuation each. They were not US dollars or any that I have seen in media reports like the Yen or Euro, but completely new.

I have already written about a currency reset for the world as per Christine Lagarde of the IMF. So I believe an imminent currency reset which was proposed, is about to take place soon.

7/16/2020

The Lord spoke from Numbers 16 vs. 46 that "The plague has begun."

The Ten Commandments of God were desecrated, so the ten plagues or judgements of God are now in play upon the world. Covid 19 will be followed by other viral diseases but I believe Bubonic plague will be one to come upon the USA. Squirrels, rabbits have already been identified as carriers of this inside the USA. Lyme disease is also common among wildlife. God's Word declares in Revelation 6 vs. 8. that the beasts of the field will be one of the major factors in the massive amounts of people dying (25% of the world's population).

7/17/2020

The voice of the Lord spoke to me and said,

As Esau gave away his Birthright for a bowl of stew, so will the USA give away their cherished rugged individuality, freedom and self worth for a man made assurance of safety and protection from pestilences, plagues, just like they have done to be protected against terrorism. The USA has thereby placed itself on the homestretch of self destruction by it's evil actions and casting aside their only protection, Jesus. Mask wearers are being pitted in bitter rage against anti maskers, and now the major stores have announced that to enter their doors, masks must be worn. Just as the Bible declares that no one will be able to buy or sell without the mark of the beast, in one day most major retail stores have announced that having no mask on, equals no entry to buy or sell, display your products, in their stores. **Mask wearing cannot hide one from the judgements of a Holy God.** The Lord has spoken and said, "The plagues are surely coming, they will come from my agents that your masks will never stop like lice, gnats, fleas, ticks, God's mighty army of the locusts, the caterpillar, cankerworm and the palmer worm just as He has done before. So what will a mandatory mask do at that time?" Repentance is what's needed for security from plagues.

Power has now been taken over by the combined corporations, unelected super wealthy ruling oligarchs and corporations to make decisions for the whole nation without the input of the elected representatives of the masses of the people, thereby usurping the right and will of the people. Major corporations have now combined in power and begun to run the governments of the world, dictating their do's and don't policies. Here's how to fight back, let the battle be The Lord's;

WEAPONIZING GOD"S WORD
Becoming a 109'er–Declaring 7 Times or more each day Psalm 109, a Weaponized Word that turns back to the sender all their fiery arrows and evil curses. Fight the 'assembly of the wicked' Ultimate Babylon New World Order wicked.

It's either you release the Word, the fire of God, or the word will be released over you, satan's words, curses of witches and warlocks unleashed upon you.

The satanic Babylonian ten percenters have banded together to bring their Agenda 21, new world order, new Babylon, upon the whole world, but what if the Christians respond by praying the same prayer before the Righteous Judge, His WORD, the same Word all at different times in every 24 hours 7 days a week, what do you believe Jesus would do? How would He respond?

Answer the same way He responded when the Church prayed without ceasing and He sent an Angel to rescue Peter from the prison (Acts 12). How many prayers were made for James?... 0, result, he was butchered by Herod. How many prayers were made for Peter? Tons, very many non stop prayers made by the Church, results, God sent an angel, the angel delivered Peter out of the prison miraculously, not a hair harmed.

Make a resolution of your will, I will not have idle angels sitting doing nothing in heaven while I am suffering here on earth. Angels neither slumber nor sleep, but I need sleep, and when I sleep I assign my angels to take charge over me and keep me and bear me up in their hands, then I go to bed and sleep.

What shall we then say to these great tribulation things that have come so suddenly upon the earth, to these fiery trials that have come to try us, a response must be given. These things must be spoken to as these things have a demonic entity behind them controlling them and their intended effects.

Romans 8, vs. 31, **"If God be for us, then who can be against us?"**

What if we all prayed Psalm 109 as our combined response, the same Psalm David prayed and prophecied against Judas, the Jesus betrayer who for 30 pieces of silver sold out Jesus, how would Jesus respond to these prayers? The same thing He did when Judas returned the money and hung himself. Judas was filled with remorse, sorrow, deep regret and did what he did, hung himself. Goodbye to bad rubbish.

After walking with Jesus he should have learned about Jesus's forgiveness and plugged into it but, satan was entrenched in him. Modern day Judases are still looking to sellout and kill Jesus by killing the carriers of Jesus Christ, his believers who carry this precious treasure in earthen vessels, our bodies. Cain is still seeking to kill the righteous Abels of this modern world, because Cain can't see God so he will seek to kill who he can see that carries God inside them, and whose worship is received by God, that's the Christians, you and me. Somebody will die but surely not me, I shall live and not die, and declare the glory of Jesus in the land of the living. I will destroy them before they destroy me.

Lets make a plan, here it is, don't allow yourself to be dumped or downloaded upon by the wicked, but you and I begin to download, transmit upon the wicked violently, let's all become **Psalm 109'ers.** Christians who are always reading audibly, **CODING**, this portion of scripture 7 Times or more per day and see God perform His Word, for he watches over only His Word to perform it. We also do it 7 times daily for His righteous Judgements to be unleashed upon the wicked. Let the BIBLE CODE 7 revolution begin now. Also according to the Word of God, any thing we set our hearts to do, just like the Babylon worshippers, we can and will accomplish. This is a moving in one accord, unison prayers, this is a spiritual plan of action, this is a response to God's invitation to call unto Him and allow Him to answer us and demonstrate His might and power to us. He will surely respond with fire and fury. Destroy the wicked by prayer and fasting before they destroy us.

Let us never forget that God watches over His WORD, only, to perform it. This is part of God's endurance plan for the believers to go through the great tribulation era that we are now in and be saved. **So let's go, let's do it! Let's not become a part of the obedient slaves to the ultimate new world satanic order, new Babylon, but a Psalm 109'er and endure till Jesus returns for us His children. AMEN.**

In God's eyes, everything equals one thing, hell or the final destination of Jesus Christ heaven, not luxury mansions, luxury lifestyles or bunkers. Not even names of Churches or denominations, but Jesus Christ alone as the greatest fingers of death and hell are about to be released upon the face of the earth. For the Christians the Word of God is our vaccines, the Word is our everything and through His Word we send back every curse and evil word spoken against us back to the sender. Our job #1 is to survive and endure till Jesus returns for us in the rapture. Never forget this.

The President and many wealthy ten percenters have a secret bunker, but God can penetrate their bunkers at any time, but who can penetrate the secret place of the most High God's bunker, who can penetrate the blood of Jesus Christ the bullet-proofed, armor plated secret bunker of God's precious people?

Genesis 11:6-7

6 And the Lord said, Behold, the people is one, and they have all one language; and this they begin to do: and now nothing will be restrained from them, which they have imagined to do.

7 Go to, let us go down, and there confound their language, that they may not understand one another's speech.

A Warning about using blood in rituals.

Jesus instructed His disciples in St. John 6, that He was the bread of life come down from heaven and that He, His flesh and body was to be eaten, without doing this we would not have eternal life, nor any part or association in Him;

St. John 6 New living Translation

53So Jesus said again, "I tell you the truth, unless you eat the flesh of the Son of Man and drink his blood, you cannot have eternal life within you. 54But anyone who eats my flesh and drinks my blood has eternal life, and I will raise that person at the last day. 55For my flesh is true food, and my blood is true drink. 56Anyone who eats my flesh and drinks my blood remains in me, and I in him.

***Jesus did not mean this literally, as His body would not be enough to go around for all people. But look how Jesus explained it at the last supper.

1 Corinthians 11 New Living Translation

23For I pass on to you what I received from the Lord himself. On the night when he was betrayed, the Lord Jesus took some bread 24and gave thanks to God for it. Then he broke it in pieces and said, "This is my body, which is given for you.*f* Do this in remembrance of me." 25In the same way, he took the cup of wine after supper, saying, "This cup is the new covenant between God and his people—an agreement confirmed with my blood. Do this in remembrance of me as often as you drink it." 26For every time you eat this bread and drink this cup, you are announcing the Lord's death until he comes again.

***Now note that the piece of bread Jesus picked up and used was like any other piece of home made bread. He pronounced over the bread a dedication or command to become His body upon being taken at the last supper rites. So upon doing so today the communion wafer and grape juice becomes as Jesus declared, His body and blood, because Jesus said so.

Now the Bible declares to us that we should not eat meats sacrificed to idols because it is spoken over, in imitation style by the devils agents, priests.

Covid 19 is real and deadly, with the only way to deal with it is attacking it's demonic spiritual component through prayer, the Word of God and blood of Jesus, the communion cup.

Acts 15 vs. 29.
Christian Standard Bible

that you abstain from food offered to idols, from blood, from eating anything that has been strangled, and from sexual immorality. You will do well if you keep yourselves from these things. Farewell."

The evil dedication makes these foods not fit for Christian consumption so they are not to be consumed if we know that this has been done, however if not then make sure to bless your foods before you eat it.

Satan now seeks to bring the ultimate deception to the Christian believers and the world, the mark of the beast, his mark without which no one can buy or sell. This mark will be inserted in the right hand or forehead, and I believe it will be done deceptively. Will it be by a microscopic molecular vaccine insertion deception?

Be warned, all readers, get a pocket paper Bible and have it ready at all times. A pocket paper BIBLE. Do not depend upon the internet, your devices they might not be available to you or the internet Bibles may be contaminated, corrupted, altered online. Nevertheless, press on with your paper bible declaring, reciting the sworn promises, the Word of God.

Be very prepared, this scriptural reference is to the USA again, the land of 'wings' aircraft, helicopters and drones, slaughter bots (mini drones made to destroy and kill do your own internet search on this) Even though Ethiopia is mentioned by the Bible printers, the message fits the muscular USA, certainly not puny Ethiopia;

Isaiah 18
New American Standard Bible
Message to Ethiopia

1Alas, oh land of whirring wings
Which lies beyond the rivers of Cush,
2Which sends envoys by the sea,
Even in papyrus vessels on the surface of the waters.
Go, swift messengers, to a nation tall and smooth,
To a people feared far and wide,
A powerful and oppressive nation
Whose land the rivers divide.
3All you inhabitants of the world and dwellers on earth,
As soon as a standard is raised on the mountains, you will see it,
And as soon as the trumpet is blown, you will hear it.
4For thus the LORD has told me,
"I will look from My dwelling place quietly
Like dazzling heat in the sunshine,
Like a cloud of dew in the heat of harvest."
5For before the harvest, as soon as the bud blossoms
And the flower becomes a ripening grape,

Then He will cut off the sprigs with pruning knives
And remove and cut away the spreading branches.
6They will be left together for mountain birds of prey,
And for the beasts of the earth;
And the birds of prey will spend the summer feeding on them,
And all the beasts of the earth will spend harvest time on them.
7At that time a gift of homage will be brought to the LORD of hosts
From a people tall and smooth,
Even from a people feared far and wide,
A powerful and oppressive nation,
Whose land the rivers divide—
To the place of the name of the LORD of hosts, even Mount Zion.

Chapter 3

U.N. Agenda 2021, The New World Order, 'Ultimate One World Babylon'.

From the satanic U.N. roundtable, the master plan for the worldwide social re-engineering agenda.
Desperately wicked hearts comprise the "assembly of the wicked".

The assembly of the wicked are gathered to do the bidding of the wicked one, satan. Satan's desire is rooted in their hearts because they are his seed. Even if a believer in Jesus is among them, they are outnumbered and outvoted usually 10-1. So the ultimate outcome is that satan and his agenda will proliferate and predominate. The increasing and encroaching darkness has almost covered the earth and gross darkness is now covering the rich that rules over the poor of the earth. Heinous and bloody decisions will be made as a final move to hand the earth over to satan for his moment of fame is coming on cue. The attempt will be to encircle and suffocate the Christians and seek their removal from the earth through governmental rules and regulations coming from wicked and deceitful hearts banded together to become the **"assembly of the wicked"**;

Jeremiah 17:9

9 The heart is deceitful above all things, and desperately wicked: who can know it?

Psalm 22:16

16 For dogs have compassed me: the assembly of the wicked have inclosed me: they pierced my hands and my feet.

As a Christian, do you love a good fight? A bloody brawl? A knockdown drag out dirty brawl that is rigged in your favor with you as the designated winner, champion and last person left standing?

Well if you don't, then get woke and love it, because you will be having one soon. Your very life will depend upon the outcome of this warfare you wage, but Jesus has already designated you the winner, if and only if you will engage the enemy in hostile Word warfare through BIBLE CODE 7. You must war a good warfare. Just as the earth exerts a strong gravitational pull upon all physical things downwards, so is the devil's strong constant gravitational pull to sin against God, to cause people to go with the flow, to follow the crowd and to descend into his lair called hell. This strong pull downwards is always exerting it's influence over all mankind and must be fought against with every ounce of our strength and being. We must fight to go upstream in a downstream world as down stream societal pressures living, lifestyles will sweep us away to the fires of hell as bad rubbish. The assembly of the wicked is in charge of the world's governments and are exerting their anti Jesus force right now.

An imperial edict has been issued, close down all your small businesses, Churches, gatherings in your Towns, Cities, State, Countries, and globally. Leave only the major corporate box and chains stores open. If you don't you'll be fined and arrested for non compliance. The Swedes were the only dissenters, because they knew the had to achieve Herd Immunity Threshold. (ABC News May 27, 2020; Sweden stayed open during coronavirus pandemic).

Welcome to **GLOBAL GOVERNANCE** and even though done by individual Mayors, Governors and other leaders across the many different nations of the world, it is being done in lock step fashion as the Agenda 2021 timeline to begin is being tracked carefully. This is a diabolically hatched worldwide scheme. This is called control by fear, management by crisis, the dialectic, not being given critical quality information, or done by option, but by edict. Let the world know that people die from infections, but not with infections, and only sick people should be quarantined, not healthy people. Covid breaks all rules, Covid patients are now dying with the infection and it's being labeled a Covid death.

Whenever and wherever man has placed his hands upon the things of the world to take control of it, thereby taking control from God, God will respond angrily and viciously. He will never give His glory to man. Man has engineered a diabolical plan to take control of the workings and people of the earth, to change times and seasons, to terminate populations, spread diseases, enslave mankind in bondage, restrict freedom of men to worship Jesus, and eventually place a man indwelt by satan to be worshipped upon earth. God will angrily

59

powerfully respond, as men take deeper roots in their plans, God will respond harshly and viciously, with His wrath and ballistic fury. He will respond with acts of God all over the world, but He will preserve and protect His own, His children, they will be preserved, taken care of miraculously, just as in the biblical days of the Ten Plagues of Egypt, He is the same God and will do it again.

Only sick people should be quarantined, isolated, not healthy people.
Leviticus 13
A real virus, but a planned response.

> 3The priest shall examine the sore, and if the hairs in it have turned white and the sore appears to be deeper than the surrounding skin, it is a dreaded skin disease, and the priest shall pronounce you unclean. 4But if the sore is white and does not appear to be deeper than the skin around it and the hairs have not turned white, the priest shall isolate you for seven days. 5The priest shall examine you again on the seventh day, and if in his opinion the sore looks the same and has not spread, he shall isolate you for another seven days.

Biblical social, stay at a distance, quarantine is for the sick people only.
Luke 17

These ten lepers knew the rules stay away from the healthy population, stand at a distance.

> 12As He entered a village, 10 men with serious skin diseasesx met Him. They stood at a distance 13and raised their voices, saying, "Jesus, Master, have mercy on us! "

Is Covid 19, an engineered bio–weapon, using nano bots (farfetched scientific robotic realities) hidden in plain sight? My questions might look foolish to those who do not read and research like I do. Condensing my research with the Lord's leading, I ask you to look at this definition of nano medicine from **Merriam Webster's Dictionary** and see clearly, read now with understanding;

<u>Did You Know?</u>

Nanotechnology, or nanotech for short, deals with matter at a level that most of us find hard to imagine, since it involves objects with dimensions of 100 billionths of a meter (1/800th of the thickness of a human hair) or less. The chemical and physical properties of materials often change greatly at this scale. Nanotechnology is already being used in automobile tires, land-mine detectors, and computer disk drives. <u>Nanomedicine is a particularly exciting field: Imagine particles the size of a blood cell that could be released into the bloodstream to form into tiny robots and attack cancer cells, or "machines" the size of a molecule that could actually repair the damaged interiors of individual cells.</u>

— *<u>The advancement of man through the modification of the human body with nanotechnology; development of nanomaterials used in electronics, structural materials,</u>*
— *<u>it increases the risk of inhalation that can severely damage lungs and could also lead to fatal health issues. It increases the risk of damaging the lungs if nanoparticles are inhaled for 60 seconds.</u>*

***My note; Engineered to form tiny remotely controllable robots or machines to attack whatever they are programmed to attack, just like tiny robot soldiers. Even the interiors of individual cells? Yes. These are the same size of the cells they are sent to attack. These are like microscopic soldiers sent on a search and destroy mission. Nano bots are like sleeper cells, or like time release capsules in the human body controlled from the internet, the cloud to act, repair, release it's payload and destroy on command. Sounds farfetched, but real.

Nano bots can be inhaled, enter the lungs and begin to release it's payload.

Just like Covid 19 is doing in the human bodies it invades right now. Farfetched yes, hard to believe, yes, but real, do your own internet search on nano bots now, get off social media for awhile and get aware of what's happening now. Be informed, the limits of possibilities are there, and it's old technology from ten to twenty years ago.

(Check out nano technology and begin to see it's advancements even in trading stocks on the stock market.)

Warning; Twenty five percent of the world's population, Two billion people are about to die shortly. Nano bots with payloads will possibly be used.

The world will convulse, with and be wracked in turmoil, pain, anguish and great distress as the birth pangs unfold across the nations of the world. No one will escape, neither the poor nor the wealthy, as no one can hide from the presence of God. **We can however hide *in* the presence of God,**

in the secret place of the most high, in the Word of God, as His Word is a shield about us, but never from His presence. The rich can hide in a bunker under the earth which they will do, however they will not know God's timing when to hide, or if Jesus will open up the earth by earthquake and swallow their bunkers deeper in the bowels of the earth making a tomb out of it. Jesus can also convey by angels the very viruses and bacteria killing the masses into their sanitized bunkers, contaminate by angelic miracles their stored foods and potable water, they have a rude awakening coming, in trying to defy the everlasting Jesus.

The Bible is inerrant, never wrong and declares that these things will come upon the earth. This is an engineered plan of the globalists to depopulate the earth, set up re education camps for sensitivity trainings of Christians and others to worship satan, and a kickoff or start date must be set and has been set.

The command has been issued, the orders have gone out, it has begun and is happening right now.

All of what is happening now July 2020 is the lead up to the great kickoff to achieve this grand master plan, a methodology or strategy must be adopted and so these vaccines, viruses, wars, famines among other devices and strategies must be utilized. Tying in God's Word and the master plan of the globalist world rulers makes it clearer for the understanding. This definition of nano medicines and technology of many years ago proves that microscopic robotic killers can be and is deployed to kill, destroy individuals and populations. Twenty five percent of the whole world's population will die from, plagues, viruses, hunger, beasts of the earth says the Bible, and note that the words **"Power was given unto them".** This power was given by Jesus to the satanic globalists to do as they want, but Jesus has assigned His angels in charge over His children to watch over them, for their security and protection in these great tribulation times, however if His children are not aware of this assignment, knowledge and how to war a good warfare, they will succumb to the deceits and agenda of satan. Hence my assignment to write this book and other books to warn them that they will be destroyed for lack of knowledge;

Hosea 4;6

6My people are destroyed for lack of knowledge: because thou hast rejected knowledge, I will also reject thee, that thou shalt be no priest to me: seeing thou hast forgotten the law of thy God, I will also forget thy children.

***Wise as serpents, in the same manner, just like a serpent. Gather serpentine wisdom, know the methodologies of satan, his wiles, tricks, deceits, strategies, study satan's modus operandi, know his warfare strategies so you will not be ambushed by them. However be harmless as doves, not venomous as a snake to physically harm or kill anyone.

Warning.. do not be destroyed for your lack of knowledge of these satanic strategies.

Matthew 10:16

16 Behold, I send you forth as sheep in the midst of wolves: be ye therefore wise as serpents, and harmless as doves.

***Jesus is the Judge of all the earth not God the Father, but Jesus the Son and must be honored just as God the Father;

John 5:22-23

22 For the Father judgeth no man, but hath committed all judgment unto the Son:
23 That all men should honour the Son, even as they honour the Father. He that honoureth not the Son honoureth not the Father which hath sent him.

It must be known and told that nothing will happen without ultimately Jesus allowing it to happen, all throughout the Bible this has been so, the desires of men has been done by them for good or evil, but in the end Jesus always triumphantly prevails. This is seen in scripture here;

Revelation6

7And when he had opened the fourth seal, I heard the voice of the fourth beast say, Come and see. 8And I looked, and behold a pale horse: and his name that sat on him was Death, and Hell followed with him. And power was given unto them over the fourth part of the earth, to kill with sword, and with hunger, and with death, and with the beasts of the earth.

***Again, Power given unto them over the fourth part of the earth, **25%** of the world's population, approximately 2 billion souls to destroy them by death with hell following. Hell is never full, it only enlarges itself to accommodate more.

From a world population.org article; their topic;
'Current Population is three times (3x) the Sustainable Level'

"Evidence of unsustainable resource use is all around us. Global aquifers are being pumped 3.5 times faster than rainfall can naturally recharge them.2 As they run dry hundreds of millions will suffer. Topsoil is being lost 10-40 times faster than it is formed.3 Feeding all 7+ billion of us will become increasingly difficult. Oceans are overfished, and a primary protein source for over 2 billion people is in jeopardy.4 Worldwide, we have lost 60% of the vertebrate species in the air, water, and land since 1970.5 How many more species can we lose and

how many more ecosystems can we destroy before humanity's own existence is threatened?"

***My note; This is the clamor for population reduction because worldwide population is **un sustainable** at this current level in their estimations. The world is therefore unmanageable, ungovernable by them so reducing population is increasing the manageability and sustainability in their rationalizations. The God given, God managed ecosystems must be taken over by men and managed by men for men and not God. God the giver and sustainer of life is now rudely shoved aside and the power to take life is now commandeered by men.

Novel (new) Corona virus. (Source; WHO)

The word "novel" indicates a "new pathogen of a previously known type" (i.e. known family) of virus. Use of the word conforms to best practices for naming new infectious diseases published by the World Health Organization (WHO).

***My notes,** Some great and logical questions about Covid 19 a real engineered virus, with a planned response, are begging for some serious answers, which by asking for these answers in light of what is going on in the world today is totally acceptable. Every news story, every update, every research on this virus must be studied to get something new about this unprecedented novel (new) strange virus. Is this Corona virus a well intended, planned, engineered biological warfare agent? Is this virus a nano medical agent released on the world to do a specific job of mass killing? Is this virus containing very minute microscopic Artificial Intelligence robots (nano bots) controlled by outside means? Is this virus a one way in no way out virus that cannot be destroyed by natural medical applications? This virus is changing, shifting mutating as has never happened before in the history of viral studies, is there a demonic component to this behavior? Is there a non natural component to it, is it a programmed robot or machine virus just as the definition and example of nano medicine gave? Different strains of Covid 19 exhibit different manifestations, is this so by nano programming or design?

Six different types have been identified. This virus affects and changes many organs in the human body, is this targeted to some groups of people? This virus acts as if it has a mind of it's own, is this virus of an intelligent design from an intelligent designer? Again is this a race specific race targeted biological Killer as African Americans are disproportionately being victims of it? Massive internal bleeding, shattering of the blood vessels, is found in African Americans, while not so much so in other racial groups, why?

The average age of Covid 19 victims are 78 years old, is this virus also age specific? Finally, why are the antibodies, the residual fighters that remain in the human body to fight the disease if it should come back again, why are these antibodies fading so fast and not being effective, or long lasting as they should naturally be?

In spite of all the publicity of Covid 19, it so far has not been as virulent as talked about. Looking at "empirical data from the CDC" it shows that "COVID has a death rate of around 0.26% – about the same rate as a tough flu year, with the average age of the victims at 78 years old.

I wrote previously about a specific targeted killer, ingestible, that destroys it's victim like lawn weed and feed that destroys lawn weeds but feeds the grass, is this it? Just like many branded **Malt Liquor** sold in the African American communities that destroys the **"worth"** of the African American men and women that drink it, is this virus to destroy the life of it's victims so as to make it not worth living?

Nothing of this nature has ever occurred since the beginning of this world until now on a worldwide basis, this is how we know that the world has entered the great tribulation era.

To further your understanding of this lab engineered virus, let's see what media is saying about this pathogen, Covid 19

Gain of function means = Studies, or research that improves the ability of a pathogen to cause disease,

The express.co.uk. Headline;

Coronavirus study identifies 'gain of function' for efficient spread in humans.

CORONAVIRUS scientists have identified a "gain of function" in the virus, which has allowed for the "efficient spread in humans," a bombshell study revealed.

By Callum Hoare PUBLISHED: 09:41, Tue, Mar 10, 2020 | UPDATED: 12:50, Thu, Mar 12, 2020

******My note** ; the virus Covid 19 has been 'gain of function' engineered, manipulated, souped up, tweaked up to be a deadly nano medical robot delivered killer virus in the lab. This nano medical payload can be delivered into the human body and build up, accumulate to a certain threshold level then do it's job in tipping the scales to destroy the Human DNA.

Merriam Webster's Dictionary definition of Artificial Intelligence;

: an area of computer science that deals with giving machines the ability to seem like they have human intelligence
: the power of a machine to copy intelligent human behavior

H I T = Herd Immunity Threshold is not even near.

Herd immunity definition = the immunity or resistance to a particular infection that occurs in a group of people or animals when a very high percentage of individuals have been vaccinated or previously exposed to the infection.

NANO ROBOTS or artificial intelligence NANO BOTS with virus payloads are farfetched, but real not science fiction. Whatever the minds of man can conceive and believe it can achieve.

Source; Interestingengineering.com April 25, 2017

In the next 10 or so years, your blood will probably be streaming with tiny nanorobots there to help keep you from getting sick or even transmit your thoughts to a wireless cloud. They will travel inside of you, on a molecular level, protecting the biological system and ensuring that you have a good and long life. The future is closer than you may think.

Nano as a term is no longer perceived as special; we got used to small devices and artificial intelligence in our daily life. Tech has developed significantly and so have potential applications of these microscopic machines.

Google's director of engineering, Ray Kurzweil, is an avid predictor of future events and claims to have a fairly high accuracy rate. He is one of the biggest proponents of the notion that nanobots will be streaming through our blood in the near future. The idea surrounding this prediction isn't that far off from modern technology.

*****My notes;** get very used to this very real term AI nano bots with a payload for this is what is at work now. Transmitted and controlled from the internet, the cloud. the future is here already unannounced. Could this virus then have been sprayed from the air as just about all nations have some victims of this nano bots?

Covid 19 virus is a real and deadly killer, and many people have already succumbed to it's ravages in death or bodily injury, especially the targeted seniors, the average age of death being 78 years old. The worldwide costs have already been calculated and taken into account of the disease and the repercussions of the global shutdown, as nothing happens by chance, but is planned and diabolically executed diligently and with a methodical precision strike. Man has calculated and planned, but God has mightier and superior plans and calculations.

Note carefully that mass media are talking loudly about "The lost year."

The second wave of Covid 19 is here and even though it's summertime, this virus is not acting like a normal virus in the summer heat at all, something is very questionable, it seems like this virus has a mind of it's own, or is being remotely controlled like a smart bio weapon, nano robot by an outside source. From the open source dictionary definitions above, I believe that the world has an engineered well controlled renegade nano robot with a virus component on it's hands, the plan of some evil minds to wreak havoc worldwide and depopulate the world by overwhelming the immune system of it's victims.

I have used my research capabilities from open source information led by the Holy Spirit to put the pieces together, connect the dots and bring this information to the people of God.

The statistics on the Covid 19 are manipulated and highly secretive, this being the complaint from many media outlets. The infection to death ratios as of now are smaller than many other routine seasonal infections, but I predict will rise a little more as I now believe this is a controlled robotic nano bio warfare virus. It is now one death per two hundred infections or less. It is also reported that many people who sign up to be tested but could not wait on the long lines and left without being tested, have received emails or other messages that they were found to be positive of the Covid 19. Also reported is the fact that a young motorcyclist was killed in an accident, death by trauma, the death report, Covid 19. The death numbers are being deliberately manipulated to bump them upwards.

People either die from diseases, or with diseases and those who died from other causes but with a touch of Covid are being labelled Covid deaths.

It is so extremely obvious that the mass media have gleefully hyped the daily story to the max about Covid 19 and the fallout over it's handling, never ceasing to scream so loudly and blatantly about how many will die from it out of this engineered pandemic. The fear engines are revving hard and loud. Many other epidemiologists have made their opinions and research known that this virus is the result of a lab ENGINEERED RNA Virus called Covid 19 for which there is no vaccine for such, but very great control of the nations and the masses by fear is working very well. Fear and confusion is the order of the day and the key whip, driver of the masses.

Covid 19 is said not to be a totally naturally occurring physiological virus, but a lab engineered demonic entity, a product that although with a natural payload component, moves under satan's robotic command and control. As a spiritual example for some people to show their allegiance to satan they drink snakes blood, human blood or animal blood in a sacrifice made to him and thereby become his possessions. Just as the grape juice and bread in our communion services become the body and blood of Jesus Christ because he said so, and we become His possessions, so do these emblems belonging to satan become his because he controls and manipulates them. God promised that the satanic things and demons will not come near our homes and bodies because we wholly belong to Him. This we believe and by faith also believe that no harm from satan's arsenal of viruses, sicknesses can overcome us. Therefore Covid 19 can never touch a BIBLE CODE 7 Word declaring Christian's body. No plague near your dwelling means no disease in your bodies, do you really believe this?

Psalm 91:9-10

9 Because thou hast made the Lord, which is my refuge, even the most High, thy habitation;
10 There shall no evil befall thee, neither shall any plague come nigh thy dwelling.

Satan controls from the clouds, using cloud technology.

Satan has already announced to the world exactly how he would achieve dominance of the world, he would 'rise above the heights of the clouds'. OK so how would this happen? Answer, cloud computing, cloud technology where he could control through supercomputers and the world controllers of the tech and internet communities. Even though satanic people dominate and control it, it still belongs to Jesus and He ultimately rules and master controls the internet. The boys that control such technology are not Jesus lovers and promoters, but satanic elites and promoters. So these nano bots are being controlled from the cloud using cloud computing. Satan will reign temporarily as a god over the whole earth of people whose names are not written in the Book of Life, yes millions will worship him, take his mark in their right hand or forehead and be lost forever in hell. It is spelled out clearly here in the Bible.

Isaiah 14:13-14

13 For thou hast said in thine heart, I will ascend into heaven, I will exalt my throne above the stars of God: I will sit also upon the mount of the congregation, in the sides of the north:

14 I will ascend above the heights of the clouds; I will be like the most High.

Just so you know the extent of scientific discoveries to do serious good or harm to the human race, i.e. depopulation, unknown to most of the masses here is some more information for you;

The power of science Source; The Guardian News (Sept. 9, 2001)

GM corn set to stop man spreading his seed

Special report: GM crops debate

Robin McKie, *science editor*

Sun 9 Sep 2001 05.49 EDT

First published on Sun 9 Sep 2001 05.49 EDT

Scientists have created the ultimate GM crop: contraceptive corn. Waiving

fields of maize may one day save the world from overpopulation.

The pregnancy prevention plants are the handiwork of the San Diego biotechnology company Epicyte, where researchers have discovered a rare class of human antibodies that attack sperm.

By isolating the genes that regulate the manufacture of these antibodies, and by putting them in corn plants, the company has created tiny horticultural factories that make contraceptives.

'We have a hothouse filled with corn plants that make anti-sperm antibodies,' said Epicyte president Mitch Hein.

'We have also created corn plants that make antibodies against the herpes virus, so we should be able to make a plant-based jelly that not only prevents pregnancy but also blocks the spread of sexual disease.'

Contraceptive corn is based on research on the rare condition, immune infertility, in which a woman makes antibodies that attack sperm.

'Essentially, the antibodies are attracted to surface receptors on the sperm,' said Hein. 'They latch on and make each sperm so heavy it cannot move forward. It just shakes about as if it was doing the lambada.'

*****My note;** If this discovery was made in 2001 and could accomplish all this, how much more advanced, targeted and refined is this technology today 2020 as we have seen a multitude of bio-tech firms start up and raise multi billions of dollars and are flourishing today. Their products and agendas have been merged with other master agendas to create a master plan so the world can be socially engineered by men to be sustainably developed and maintained in man's idea of balance.

More nano medical vaccines are coming soon;

The promise of more vaccines are more promises than can be delivered. Due to the rapidity of mutations of an RNA virus, one just cannot hit a constantly moving target. No effective vaccines can be made for this RNA manipulated virus. Know this also, that viruses can never be eradicated as we are foolishly led to believe, only their effects will fade out after HIT, Herd Immunity Threshold has been achieved.

These new coming engineered vaccines will be Lab engineered vaccines that will most likely be remotely controlled just like Covid 19, that will **rewrite the DNA** of humans injected with it. Once the life CODE, DNA, has been rewritten, these humans will then become like in the days of Noah where the genetic code, the DNA has been permanently altered. The Bible tells us that as it was in the days of Noah and Lot, so it will be like in the days when Jesus will return so we are seeing a lead up to that time by the things we see happening today.

Many politicians have been compromised, blackmailed for some indiscretion they have done and so they must be silent, shut up, regarding this bombshell information. The first order of things to come will be immunity passports or papers to travel. This will be followed by an outcry that will be a clamor for an inserted chip because of forged or false papers. Many Christians will be deceived, destroyed by lack of knowledge, led as lambs to the slaughter and take the mark of the beast, the chip, without which they cannot buy sell or travel.

Now that major industries, travel, national boundaries and economies have been shut down resulting in an economic financial pit of joblessness, homelessness, closed and bankrupt businesses, with massive poverty left in it's wake, not even the central governments of nations are debating in their governing bodies, the effects of this massive financial pit or deficit. This is a super secret as Global imperial edicts have gone out not to debate this financial condition. Keep the minds and focus of the people on Covid 19 only, not on other things, as that allows the Agenda to move forward smoothly.

The tax rates, fees, fines and penalties are about to be increased drastically worldwide upon the masses, in light of the drastic loss of revenues from the Covid 19 lockdowns, the end result will be the financial oppression of the poor and working class masses now more than ever before. Saddling them with more debt, fines and penalties, financial burdens. The police will be used to issue citations, fines, court appearances for not wearing masks and other infractions of social distancing, while the other more important crimes will go unheeded. This additional pressure on the masses will make more people commit suicides, murders and other heinous crimes. Those hired and sworn to protect and serve will become the very hated petty oppressors and masters of the masses, who will be invisible when really needed because writing tickets brings more money in government coffers than fighting crime and investigating criminals. This will become a key talking point for the defunding of the aggressive petty mask police. Again, the misery index USA must be upped drastically to fit the Agenda. This is the way it must be, because the timetable to begin Agenda 2021, must be kept, total obedience to the globalists is demanded, the whole world and systems must be reset to fit the final new world order ultimate global Babylon.

But beat the drums and make a noise that shutting down the global economy does not intimidate or destroy the coronavirus, but helps the virus spread by making people poorer, and having no money to buy foods, medicines, doctors services, pay mortgages and rent, many in the masses will become malnourished, more stressed, sicker and succumb quicker to the ravages of the disease because of a deficient immunological system while living on the streets or in wooded areas in tents. Another shutdown suggested by expert **educated fools** with their little computer models in the name of the science god will be the right hook to the economy, the lives and livelihoods of the masses who have already suffered the left hook of the first shutdown. The USA has lost an incredible 32.9% of GDP output in just 3 months. Another shutdown will make many

Americans already on the brink, live under the bridges and in tents in the freezing cold while these intellectual fools are well paid, comfy, warm, while fulfilling the AGENDA. Intellectual fools who have no wisdom because they don't know The Lord as Savior. Begin to use BIBLE CODE 7 warfare (Psalm 109) against these assembly of the wicked and deceitful who have enclosed the President, Senate and Congress.

Lockdowns, masks, distancing helps to isolate people from other people, bacteria and viruses, but also weakens their immune systems by not having germs to fight off constantly. Breathing in CO_2 laden air in masks will deteriorate blood O_2 levels which leads to further compromised immune systems, sicknesses and a weaker body.

Bringing the Government to become the paymaster means government gives, but now they have the right to take away also and dictate more to the recipients of such monies. They also gets the right to order the masses what to do or not do, freedoms will be taken away and a dictatorship will rise to prepare for the anti Christ, son of perdition. Once laws are made, regulations given, they are very seldom taken back to allow a return to normalcy. So preserve what freedom is left by CODING Psalm 109.

The globalists Final Solution
Re engineering the human race, trans humanism...mixing mingling man with satan's programmed computers.

Hidden in plain sight, in the public records, is a master plan concocted in 1992 and signed by 178 nations at that time concerning the whole world.

A global master plan that the masses in the world has never heard of or forgotten about and the media will not inform about. The name is AGENDA 2021. Designed under the umbrella as a climate change agenda and solution for the listed **17 Agendas** they are supposed to improve. This master plan spells out a revamping, reset of nations and attitudes of peoples. Man and satan's plan to revamp or reset the attitudes of people, to do so a dialectic must be employed. What is a dialectic?

A dialectic is what you need the people to do or where to go or behave, it's called the solution. A severe problem is created in the midst of the people, so severe that the people beg for relief or deliverance from the problem because of fear, hardship or the horrendous suffering endured. The solution is then offered or implemented as the way out, take the solution or stay in the problem. The masses will then gladly or even grudgingly beg to take it, this solves the problem and the proposed solution is thereby adopted. This is how to force an attitude change upon the masses, like it or not, using the whip of fear, confusion and terror.

This Agenda 21 is not of God, as Jesus was not invoked at this Babylon world gathering in 1992, and man cannot legislate involuntary changes to people's attitudes and behavior without Jesus. A coming together of all nations in this manner which was certainly not in the name of Jesus Christ, is similar to the coming together at Shinar, Babylon for a meeting of the minds in the first ultimate satanic one world order worship service with Preacher Nimrod. This therefore is a man designed plan just like Babylon worship and building construction in the plains of Shinar. (Gen. 11) This Agenda is a man designed plan that has great bone crushing teeth to it, great hardships, sufferings, bloodshed and death are coming from it upon the whole world. A plan to bring tremendous chaos and bloodshed upon the world, in this resetting and especially those nations and leaders that oppose this satanic agenda. The world as we know it will be changed totally, nothing will remain the same, it will be totally reset. To bring in, implement the new, the old must be burnt, discarded, done away with. Only the things of the Lord will remain, and of course His everlasting unchangeable sworn promises, His Word. This planned revolution began with the Covid 19 virus released upon the populations of the world. The master strategy, dialectic to make the world beg for a vaccine, a deliverer, hero, savior, an answer man, a way out with the solutions to the massive chaos and bloodshed that will ensue. The massive economic catastrophe, social breakdown, mass fear and hysteria, the fighting and devouring of the masses by each other, black against white, middle class against poor. All this is by satanic dialectic design. Remember that the rich rules over the poor, and borrower is slave to the lender, so keep all the masses, black, white, middle class, whatever, keep them poor, as slaves and have full control over them.

TRANS GENERATIONAL GENOME EDITING = DAYS OF NOAH.

Trans generational = Crossing over, or passing on to the next generation.

The final end, and final solution to the new world order ultimate Babylon Agenda is to do as satan did in the Book of Genesis chapter 6, own and control most of the world, where all mankind except Noah and his family, was found to be of altered genealogy, altered, tampered with in their genes- DNA, and by so doing became satan's seed. All people on earth were corrupted, gene altered, gene tampered, genetically DNA modified. Being genetically modified people, now means they belong to satan, they have been corrupted over into satan's image and likeness–perverted and corrupted as satan can never create. God's perfect creation of mankind, male and female has now been altered, corrupted, perverted, just like marriage between one man and one woman ordained by God, so that the human species can reproduce after their own kind. Just like boys trans gendering into girls, and girls into boys through surgery and hormone treatments. This alteration process is given the nice sounding name of **GENE THERAPY, GENE MODIFICATION, DESIGNER BABIES.** This is the Agenda, It's here now, thus fulfilling God's prophecied Word here;

Luke 17, Good news Translation

26 As it was in the time of Noah so shall it be in the days of the Son of Man. 27 Everybody kept on eating and drinking, and men and women married, up to the very day Noah went into the boat and the flood came and killed them all. 28 It will be as it was in the time of Lot. Everybody kept on eating and drinking, buying and selling, planting and building. 29On the day Lot left Sodom, fire and sulfur rained down from heaven and killed them all. 30That is how it will be on the day the Son of Man is revealed.

Source; History.com
Tuskegee Experiment: The Infamous Syphilis Study
Source; History.com
Tuskegee Experiment: The Infamous Syphilis Study

Known officially as the Tuskegee Study of Untreated Syphilis in the Negro Male, the study began at a time when there was no known treatment for the disease.
Elizabeth Nix,
May 16, 2017

The Tuskegee experiment began in 1932, at at a time when there was no known treatment for syphilis. After being recruited by the promise of free medical care, 600 men originally were enrolled in the project.

The participants were primarily sharecroppers, and many had never before visited a doctor. Doctors from the U.S. Public Health Service (PHS), which was running the study, informed the participants—399 men with latent syphilis and a control group of 201 others who were free of the disease—they were being treated for bad blood, a term commonly used in the area at the time to refer to a variety of ailments.

The men were monitored by health workers but only given placebos such as aspirin and mineral supplements, despite the fact penicillin became the recommended treatment for syphilis in 1947. PHS researchers convinced local physicians in Macon County not to treat the participants, and research was done at the Tuskegee Institute. (Now called Tuskegee University, the school was founded in 1881 with Booker T. Washington at its first teacher.)

In order to track the disease's full progression, researchers provided no effective care as the men died, went blind or insane or experienced other severe health problems due to their untreated syphilis.

In the mid-1960s, a PHS venereal disease investigator in San Francisco named Peter Buxton found out about the Tuskegee study and expressed his concerns to his superiors that it was unethical. In response, PHS officials formed a committee to review the study but ultimately opted to continue it, with the goal of tracking the participants until all had died, autopsies were performed and the project data could be analyzed.

As a result, Buxton leaked the story to a reporter friend, who passed it on to a fellow reporter, Jean Heller of the Associated

Press. Heller broke the story in July 1972, prompting public outrage and forcing the study to shut down.

By that time, 28 participants had perished from syphilis, 100 more had passed away from related complications, at least 40 spouses had been diagnosed with it and the disease had been passed to 19 children at birth.

People will be eating drinking going about their daily walks of life, minding their own businesses, but all these things have been happening unseen and unknown to them until the satanists are ready to make their move, but God will make a superior move, CHECKMATE. When the satanists move, they will try to cause, force, make everyone comply or die to take the mark of satan, stamp, vaccine, chip in the right hand or forehead.

There will be a stiff resistance from millions of believers in Jesus Christ however, at which point the major Corporations and businesses will chip in, no mark, no buying or selling. Today it's no mask, no entry into the stores nationwide USA, even if your State has no mandatory mask order, you must follow the stores corporate orders to purchase, and soon, no stamp, mark or chip, equals no buying no selling. Comply or starve. The Corporations have usurped the lawfully elected representatives of the State and Local Governments and become the Federal and Local law making body themselves, they now rule over all the people by their regulations. What will your response be? Are you prepared for more draconian rules? How? How will you fight this, and with what?

Genesis 6:5-13

5 And God saw that the wickedness of man was great in the earth, and that every imagination of the thoughts of his heart was only evil continually.

6 And it repented the Lord that he had made man on the earth, and it grieved him at his heart.

7 And the Lord said, I will destroy man whom I have created from the face of the earth; both man, and beast, and the creeping thing, and the fowls of the air; for it repenteth me that I have made them.

8 But Noah found grace in the eyes of the Lord.

***There will be total destruction, annihilation from the presence of God by those who take that mark which dooms them to everlasting hell with no redemption. Noah was in God's favor because his DNA was God made, perfect not altered or tampered with. This is the jealousy of God that one does not tamper with His perfect creation, or try to alter what He has perfectly made. Lungs, hearts, livers etc. can be transplanted from one human to another, but the sacred CODE of life from God must not be touched. Touching the CODE, the DNA, is touching God, and incurring His wrath, His fury.

To try even to change anything in the CODE of His creation, the DNA is a manipulation of satanic origin, yes gene altering, DNA manipulation, GM foods is satanic. The other CODE of God is His Word, which satan tampered with and thereby deceived Eve to sin by altering, changing the Word of God. Beware of the two sacred untouchable CODES, the DNA and His WORD. In Babylon worship, the Word is altered and men have sex with men and women with women and animals, the fury of God will surely descend upon them to respond for such abominations, yes He will respond for sure.

Do not do it or be involved in it, the alteration of His Word or the DNA. We as the general population are eating Genetically Modified foods and meats without even knowing it has been altered, not even knowing what will become of our third and fourth generations, our children in the future from eating these GM foods. The unzipping of our DNA is occurring at warp speed. Occasionally, there are strange media stories of animals born with human like features which are occurring with more frequency around the world. A human DNA corrupted world will be lost and totally destroyed again by God as bad rubbish, just like a branch cut off from a tree, good for nothing but to be burned in the fire as firewood. He did it before, He'll do it again, He's the same Holy God forever.

The biblical precedent is here in Genesis chapter 6, yes God is jealous over His creation, whether men are even saved or unsaved.

Now there is a plan afoot to speed up the unzipping of mankind's DNA to fulfill or fit satan's Agenda to give us over to satan unwittingly, unknowingly by stealth, it's called TRANS GENERATIONAL GENOME EDITING. How it will be done is simple, insert by a vaccine into the human body the messenger RNA agent, this RNA agent will then do the rest once into the bloodstream. Remember it'a a messenger agent sent with a command to do a certain job.

Genesis 6

9 These are the generations of Noah: Noah was a just man and perfect in his generations, and Noah walked with God.

***Noah was perfect in his generations, genealogy, meaning his DNA was perfect, untampered with, just as GOD designed it and kept it, maintained by God along with his sons and their wives DNA. The Lord identifies with what He has engineered and produced as PERFECT, because He is perfection, His creation is perfection, after He was finished with it, He saw and commented that it is 'good' because he is GOOD, no flaws are found in God neither in His creation. We are made in His Image and after His likeness. It is only our free will that He has given to us that we foolishly exercise that makes us sin against Him.

God now moves upon His perfection, His creation, mankind, Noah and family. God is now determined to save them from contamination, corruption, altering by saving Noah and all his family. God will now begin afresh through them to repopulate the earth, through these eight perfect genetic CODE made up persons, saved from the worldwide flood in the Ark, eight persons, the number of new beginnings. One day with God is like a thousand years to us humans.

God will in like manner rescue His children soon from today's contaminated and soon to be super contaminated world, before they become contaminated in their life CODE, the DNA, so get ready.

<u>WARNING: don't take the vaccines, Do not allow any mark or chip to be inserted in you at any cost. It is deception to destroy us and give us into satan's hand. Be ready to lose jobs, money houses lands everything, but at all costs do not take the loaded vaccines or mark of satan.</u>

10 And Noah begat three sons, Shem, Ham, and Japheth.

11 The earth also was corrupt before God, and the earth was filled with violence.

12 And God looked upon the earth, and, behold, it was corrupt; for all flesh had corrupted his way upon the earth.

13 And God said unto Noah, The end of all flesh is come before me; for the earth is filled with violence through them; and, behold, I will destroy them with the earth.

Vaccine Makers need and gets immunity from liability. 8/2/2020

AstraZeneca to be exempt from coronavirus vaccine liability claims in most countries

Ludwig Burger

(Reuters)–AstraZeneca has been granted protection from future product liability claims related to its COVID-19 vaccine hopeful by most of the countries with which it has struck supply agreements, a senior executive told Reuters.

FILE PHOTO: The company logo for pharmaceutical company AstraZeneca is displayed on a screen on the floor at the New York Stock Exchange (NYSE) in New York, U.S., April 8, 2019. REUTERS/Brendan McDermid/File Photo

With 25 companies testing their vaccine candidates on humans and getting ready to immunize hundred millions of people once the products are shown to work, the question of who pays for any claims for damages in case of side effects has been a tricky point in supply negotiations.

"This is a unique situation where we as a company simply cannot take the risk if in ... four years the vaccine is showing side effects," Ruud Dobber, a member of Astra's senior executive team, told Reuters.

"In the contracts we have in place, we are asking for indemnification. For most countries it is acceptable to take that risk on their shoulders because it is in their national interest," he said, adding that Astra and regulators were making safety and tolerability a top priority.

Dobber would not name the countries.

EU officials told Reuters this week product liability was among contentious points in European efforts to secure supply deals for potential COVID-19 vaccines from Pfizer, Sanofi and Johnson & Johnson.

The United States, however, already has a law to exclude tort claims from products that help control a public-health crises in the form of the 2005 Public Readiness and Emergency Preparedness, or PREP Act.

*****My note**, These bio tech companies rushing new improperly tested patented messenger RNA vaccines, not knowing fully all the complications to be encountered, shows that there is an agenda and a deadline to meet. These RNA vaccines have never been used on humans before, properly rigorously tested, so they do not know the full effects of these vaccines.

Anything that is patented is owned by the one who patented it, which means that if it is foods, new life giving substances, it has been altered genetically and if altered it will also alter a person's DNA. **Natural things cannot be patented, it must be altered first then patented.** Can these new patented RNA vaccines be called a bio weapon?

On the frontline of this Covid battle are frontline doctors who know from their preventive medical encounters with their patients and the disease what works and doesn't work to save lives. Yet these doctors are being maligned and verbally abused by spokesmen, office administrators, government agency heads combined with an unelected and non medical powerful billionaire influential spokesman being told what to do and not to do for **giving their testimonials of their experiences** of what does and does not work. The cherished privacy and confidence of a doctor patient relationship has been shattered by the Governmental authorities who demand that doctors not use proven drugs that have been used for over sixty years worldwide anymore, but to use unproven new drugs that haven't been proven to work.

The frontline doctors with experience and knowledge are being silenced, shut down by these deceitful hearts of wickedness and evil, labeled as people in white lab coats, what an act of obvious defamation, but the blood of Jesus be against these assembly of wicked, deceitful people that have inclosed them and seeks to shut them up. The fire and fury of God be against them, let God arise and scatter them in confusion.

Our lives are too precious and important to us to trust these deceitful and wicked minds. Self preservation and self defenses must now kick in by refusing this rushed unproven unworkable foreign intrusion into our personal bodies, these patented new RNA vaccines. Our bodies belong to us, we own our bodies, this is our most treasured asset along with our very souls, we are conscientious and religious objectors to these violations and intrusions of our most sacred and precious possession, our very own bodies. So again I recommend, NO CHIPS, NO VACCINES INTO OUR BODIES. Stand and fight, plead the BLOOD of JESUS against the wicked people.

My prayer is whatever the assembly of wicked and deceitful minds sows in this vaccine agenda, just like the Bible character Haman, the man who sought to kill Mordecai, so shall they and their families must also <u>instantly</u> reap.

<u>Gene editing, manipulations, Source: National Human Genome Research Institute. genome.gov</u>

So as to give you a basic understanding and to inform you of the current status of today's research and scientific capabilities, I give this information from this U.S. Government source here :

While the popular media tends to focus on the potential use of genome editing in humans, the main application of this technology has been in basic research. Editing the genomes of yeast, bacteria, mice, zebrafish, and other organisms that scientists commonly study has led to countless discoveries about how the genome is connected to physical traits, like eye color, and disease.

Researchers funded by the National Human Genome Research Institute (NHGRI) and other research institutes at the National Institutes of Health (NIH) are adopting newer techniques, such as CRISPR, to conduct their investigations. A robust understanding of how the genome gives rise to health and disease will aid the development of new treatments, including **gene therapy**.

***My note, (Please note the word ; gene therapy, highlight is not mine).

Genome Editing Methods

Scientists have had the knowledge and ability to edit genomes for many years, but CRISPR technology has brought major improvements to the speed, cost, accuracy, and efficiency of genome editing. The history of genome editing technologies shows the remarkable progress in this field and also relays the critical role that basic science research plays in the development of research tools and potential disease treatments.

***My note, all this taken from open source websites to inform of the lateness of the hour, the most advanced and latest mind blowing scientific technologies and capabilities being used, that man is now playing God on earth, and as in Noah's days they have gone down to the genetic CODE, DNA levels, the very microscopic molecular building blocks of life, to socially re- engineer almost all mankind by stealth, deception, against their knowledge and will if possible, into satan's image and likeness, to alter, change, corrupt mankind who is made in the image and likeness of God.

Resist through BIBLE CODE 7.

Covid 19 is the attention grabber, but sin is the problem.

Again, the time frame of AGENDA 21 to be in action must be kept.

As a result of the recent Covid 19 lockdowns, a little over 1 billion people worldwide are very close to starvation, food insecurity, evictions and losing all their earthly possessions. The financial repercussions are kicking in. By the way, was this the satanic globalist's aim and intention in the first place? All eyes, all attention is now focused upon this virus, but while the media and masses attention are raging over Covid 19, many major pieces of their Agenda are being put in place, with no fanfare. Covid 19 serves as a major distraction, diversion while there is a simmering disagreement between the USA, China, Russia, Venezuela, North Korea and Iran. The Middle East Israel, Syria, Iran among others. The war drums are still beating, the temperature is still rising, but all this has been overshadowed by Covid 19.

Gold is rising, going through the roof, the US dollar falling, many nations are ditching the US dollar in trading, Oil wars and many more black swans rising.

Never let a good crisis go to waste, the world reset is still being moved along by the globalists trying to keep their schedule of 2021 to kick off the master plan. At the right time, a horrible war will break out and engulf the whole world one way or another, because of the interconnectedness of all nations.

Covid 19 is the first body blow, the first domino to soften up the whole world for acceptance of this Reset Agenda. **A massive and catastrophic displacement of populations is about to happen worldwide, with refugees or homeless people all over the world, first second and third world countries. (more fear, confusion).**

In the nursing homes, in hospitals the sick and elderly are dying and aging more rapidly, and dying more quickly for lack of seeing their children and grandchildren, loneliness kills. People are social beings, iron sharpens iron, people needs people.

With the mask regulations, only the non mask wearers can be identified by facial recognition cameras, with this in mind are they keeping a record of the non maskers, labeled as the resisters?

Could this also be a way of conditioning the masses to obey commands and the ensuing obedience training to the one percent masters new one world Babylon agenda? Yes it is, satan is always imitating God, as God calls for our obedience by voluntary submission to Him, satan calls for total submission by strong arm robbery, killing and destruction, but submit anyhow, then eventually take his mark upon your body in the right hand or forehead to show full allegiance to him.

Sustainable development means development that can be sustained or maintained and we have been warned all along by many influential governing bodies, officials and experts, that the deficit spendings, constant borrowings and debt to GDP ratios are all UN SUSTAINABLE. That population growth and the ability to feed and house so many people in the world's nations are UN SUSTAINABLE. In other words planet earth is 3 times overpopulated and that is unsustainable and the chief reason for the world's troubles. Even Prince Philip, queen Elizabeth's husband has voiced his desire after death to come back as a virus to exterminate and lower the masses in the world's population. We have been told that if we come together as one and be a one world global body and nation all will be well, things will work better and we will have a happy, peaceful glorious world with a global leader and leadership, no more sectarian strife as we will have a one world religion and all worship the same god. This is the promised utopia under satan, but remember satan can only rob, kill, destroy, pervert, or corrupt what God has so wonderfully designed and brought into manifestation.

So here we have it, the dialectic for AGENDA 2021 in full operation.

It seemed like just a few months ago that the U.S. Titanic was full steam ahead, a great economy, many jobs, low unemployment, money circulating, all was fabulously well, then suddenly it hit iceberg Covid 19, now it's limping listlessly in the tumultuous sea of uncertain recovery, tossed by it's boisterous, confusing, traitorous political winds, and battered by it's ugly waves of millions unemployed, bankruptcies, homelessness, riots, protests, suicide, drug, substance dependence, hopelessness and despair. This is not just a USA problem, but worldwide, such as never been seen since the whole world began. Welcome folks, welcome worldwide to the great tribulation, spoken of by Jesus Himself here;

Matthew 24
God's Word Translation

21There will be a lot of misery at that time, a kind of misery that has not happened from the beginning of the world until now and will certainly never happen again. **22**If God does not reduce the number of those days, no one will be saved. But those days will be reduced because of those whom God has chosen.

Elites are different, rooted in secret societies, cults.

The rich ruling class elites have a different bloodline, they are of their father the devil. They have been genetically altered, spiritually and maybe even physically, they are satan's seed, just like in the days of Noah, they are therefore not normal like us the rest of the masses. Many elites drink animal, bird, human or child's blood with the life force in it, and eat human flesh, the innocence that can be written upon in this blood force is evilly powerful. This makes them in a sense evilly supernatural with a demonic protection and force by which they control the masses not under the blood of Jesus. They demonically control, just like Simon of Samaria in the Book of Acts. The worldwide response to the coronavirus is a proclamation, a conditioning strategy that leads to blind obedience of the masses under penalty of new hastily made laws. Fear, confusion, terrorizes, and drives the herd of humanity to do the bidding of the ruling class worldwide now as this is a worldwide crisis, a real engineered virus with a planned response to it, A PLAN DEMIC.

Wake up world, it's bow or burn time, just as in the days of king Nebuchadnezzar. See here;

Daniel 3, NASB Bible

4Then the herald loudly proclaimed: "To you the command is given, O peoples, nations and men of every language, 5that at the moment you hear the sound of the horn, flute, lyre, trigon, psaltery, bagpipe and all kinds of music, you are to fall down and worship the golden image that Nebuchadnezzar the king has set up. 6"But whoever does not fall down and worship shall immediately be cast into the midst of a furnace of blazing fire."

It seems like the elites have a handle on all these things going on, even the Bible tells us that it will seem like their evil is prospering and triumphing, but God will always counter all of satan's seed and deeds, when we begin to war a good warfare. Jesus will feed them their own flesh and make them drink their own blood and be drunken by it, but he prey shall be taken out of the rich and mighty's hands and chains. All the oppressors must now drink their own blood and not that of another and devour their own flesh and not another's;

Isaiah 49:24-26

24 Shall the prey be taken from the mighty, or the lawful captive delivered?
25 But thus saith the Lord, Even the captives of the mighty shall be taken away, and the prey of the terrible shall be delivered: for I will contend with him that contendeth with thee, and I will save thy children.
26 And I will feed them that oppress thee with their own flesh; and they shall be drunken with their own blood, as with sweet wine: and all flesh shall know that I the Lord am thy Saviour and thy Redeemer, the mighty One of Jacob.

So let's recognize our moment and seize it to make war against the adversaries in self defense, and self preservation through BIBLE CODE 7, the minesweeping strategy of spiritual Word warfare.

The Davos gang and bankers of Basel, World Economic Forum.

Allow me to make this abundantly clear, the top tier wealthy ONE percenters that control 55% OF THE WORLD'S WEALTH DESIRES THE 99% WHO SCRAPE BY ON 45% OF THE WORLD'S WEALTH to be busily fighting each other to death while they laugh at our stupidity and gullibility as we are preoccupied in fighting and murdering each other, all so we cannot see or focus our attention upon them. All attention has been diverted, deflected from them to each other of the 99% like crabs in a barrel. Just below the one percenters, the other 9 % have combined with them to make ten percent. Ten percent of the worlds adult population owns and controls 85% of the world's wealth. So 90% of the world's population runs on 15% of the whole world's wealth. The great majority of the one percenters don't run the world, but however controls it. The one percenters belong to the World Economic Forum, a world body that controls the world's every economic move and now seeks to control every aspect of the masses lives, to the very extent that they will determine how many will die, (Pale horse of Revelation) demand a mark in the right hand or forehead to buy or sell and show allegiance and ownership to satan. Meeting every year in Davos Switzerland, they strategize every move to keep their rule over the poor worldwide intact. This is the final solution, to mark satan's worshippers and elim-inate Jesus's worshippers. But Jesus the great UPSETTER has a great upset for satan and his agents. Jesus still controls earth-quakes, hurricanes, floods, pestilences, plagues, even wars and fightings among men, He is still in total absolute control of every thing in this earth, the earth still belongs to Him and all people in it, even if they rebel against Him their lives are still His to dispose of. Locusts, caterpillars, cankerworms, palmer worms God refers to as His mighty army. Along with flies, lice, gnats, frogs, mosquitoes and many more Jesus is in perfect control of all aspects of mankind. Jesus can afflict the wicked and leave the righteous untouched. So take care of these bad rubbish with Psalm 109, become a 109'er.

Covid 19 has now ushered in the GREAT TRIBULATION with a bang that the Bible mentions in the Book of Matthew;

Matthew 24:21

21 For then shall be great tribulation, such as was not since the beginning of the world to this time, no, nor ever shall be.

Again, so as to cast all attention away from the real world trouble makers, the ultra rich one percenters, unknown, invisible ruling class overlords, the attention and general focus will be upon all other things as a diversion and distraction. Understand carefully that those who run the world are known by the world as they are the elected and appointed leaders that are seen, heard and known. But those that control the world are never seen or known, they are the world's trillionaires and super billionaires that belong to secret clubs and societies and may never ever be known or heard of to the masses in the world. So the remaining 90% of the world's population fight each other and scrapes by on 15% of the entire world's wealth (Source Oxfam). The ruling class now causes the 90% (the paycheck to paycheck masses) black and white and all other colors of all nationalities to be divided and always fight and grouse against each other for crumbs, as they control the lion's share of wealth, and the mass media. The masses even kill each other out of hate and jealousy, so job one of the one percenters is to keep the masses busy in divisions, diversions and strife, as they will never see the real enemy and do anything about it as their eyes are blinded and they are dumbed down stupid by the agenda of the ten percenters.

It must be noted that there are a very small amount, a few ten percenters and one percenters that follows The Lord and His Word, so references are made to the great satanic majority of them.

Get the picture? Now let's get back to the BIBLE that so many people ignore and are ignorant of and see what it says. Again, it says **the world has an ultra rich vs. ultra poor problem, a super rich vs. slave class borrowers problem.**

Proverbs 22:7

7 The rich ruleth over the poor, and the borrower is servant to the lender.

God's solution.

This begs the question, is this a loving God's plan for mankind, that the ungodly devil worshipping Babylon loving ten percenter rich rule over and oppress the poor of the world? What does God say about this? Can this be reversed? Will He hear the poor as they cry out to Him about their conditions?

The answer is there in the Bible hidden in plain sight, and revealed through BIBLE CODE 7.

This strategy was revealed in my first book, "The Hundredfold, Through BIBLE CODE 7"

There is no other way to fight the ten percenters as they have employed super warlocks and witches just like Jannes, Jambres, Balaam, and Simon Magus to bewitch the masses, keep them poor and broke, and keep themselves in great wealth, to maintain their status quo. Many have employed black money rituals, that's why they are called the black nobilities, they are satan's children. The only way to shatter and destroy their wealth, health, power and evil is with the Word of God weapon-ized through BIBLE CODE 7 strategy. Yes, there is a way out, there is a solution, the answers lie in fighting from above, the heavens, using supernatural weapons, the weapons that cannot fail but will destroy tyrants and their tyranny, the wicked and their wickedness and evil, the ungodly and their ungodliness, The Lord is never sleeping, but still renders righteous judge-ments upon calling unto Him through His Words;

Proverbs 14:20
20 The poor is hated even of his own neighbour: but the rich hath many friends.

Proverbs 28:6
6 Better is the poor that walketh in his uprightness, than he that is perverse in his ways, though he be rich.

Revelation 3:16-17
16 So then because thou art lukewarm, and neither cold nor hot, I will spue thee out of my mouth.
17 Because thou sayest, I am rich, and increased with goods, and have need of nothing; and knowest not that thou art wretched, and miserable, and poor, and blind, and naked:

So let's make this abundantly clear, the noble sounding, good intentioned gathering and plan of men, gathered from all nations of the world for a great social re engineering master plan, and gathered in a Babylon style fashion in Rio De Janeiro Brazil in 1992 without invoking the name of Jesus Christ, was adopted without any input from Jesus. This will then be forced upon the world as an agenda to be implemented by the whole world, as a ten year 'master plan,' to be thrust upon the whole world and it's population whether they like it or not, beginning in 2021. This **'agenda of the ten percenters'**, it's about to be delivered, implemented in a few months, unless...The people who know their God and authority and power in Him and His Word begin to utilize that power in the WORD of GOD through BIBLE CODE 7 Word self defense, self preservation warfare strategy. This is our only hope. War with the Word of God, to have God deliver a judgement strike upon the unrighteous, the Everlasting Judge will surely take them out and shatter their plans. They must either repent or perish.

Agenda 21 is hidden in plain sight, out of sight and out of mind. As spies and intelligence operatives are taught to do, hide every thing in plain sight as it will never be found out by the gullible dumbed down masses, so is this agenda hidden in plain sight. This agenda can be viewed by going online To: **sustainabledevelopment.un.org** —pull it up and read it for yourself. Get off social media and other time wasting things, and get busy, then when you get the big picture, turn to Jesus Christ The Lord and Savior, and after this, then begin to use the Strategy of BIBLE CODE 7 to destroy the satanic chains that tied you and make your way clear and prosperous. Now then you can get back on social media and began to inform the gullible dumbed down 90 % of what is going on.

Globalists Vs. U.S. Patriots

In what I am about to reveal, nothing political is intended on my part as I am an independent thinker, however as I have revealed in my third and fourth books, the visions that The Lord has shown me regarding U.S. President Donald Trump. This is not about your political party affiliation Democrat or Republican, this is bigger than that, this is about **The Lord's agenda** as revealed to me. Without going over the visions in full, I will reveal again that President Trump will be **valiant** and **dodge** all attempts upon his life and his presidency. President Trump will be saved by Jesus Christ in office, as in the vision that I saw, I proclaimed twice, **"This is an honest man you can trust him, this is an honest man you can trust him",** this was said after the Dodge Valiant car I was driving him in approached a large group of African American people, he jumped out and waded into the crowd shaking hands with everyone. This vision tells me President Trump will be put in office by a massive African American vote in his favor in the 2020 election.

President Trump is certainly not an honest man as of this writing July 2020, but will become an honest man after his Damascus Road encounter with Jesus Christ. Just like Apostle Paul who encountered Jesus and was mightily used of God, so will President Trump become a great tool in The Lord's hand. God will use him mightily to lead the USA back to Himself so He can extend mercy upon it for a short season.

President Trump himself and his policies presents a stumbling block to the AGENDA 21, the new world order, satanic globalists and one world government proponents. President Trump is being resisted at every turn as I saw in the second vision of him. He is being coerced, blackmailed, threatened to fall in line to this agenda, and sad to say also as seen in the vision, an attempt will be made upon his life but it will not be successful. Almost all of his chosen inner circle people, some very very close to him have viciously turned on him and betrayed him like Judas betrayed Jesus. At this point in time there are very few people that he can trust in his inner circle, and he needs desperately some confidential, trustworthy people and advisors. The advice he now receives are from bad actors, ungodly, wicked advisors who have backed him into a corner where he is now in a war zone. This unconventional war is against entrenched bureaucrats who oppose his every move and order and are trying to wait him out, hoping he will not be re elected. The deck has been stacked against him and only a second term can bring him to overcome this battle. The key weakness of President Trump is the selecting of bad ungodly advisors and key personnel, intelligent but fools, having no wisdom.

President Trump is a great U.S. Patriot, he is not a new world order, one world government satanic globalist, nor is he globalist minded, but one who dearly loves his country, (Visions from Pastor Stacy McDonald attests to this), however, I do not believe he is a born again Christian. The USA has many great patriots, those who love the USA, but many are not Jesus believing Christians. I do not judge President Trump, but I inspect the fruit of his declared salvation which is not evident in his life and presidency by the actions we have seen, heard, by words and deeds, again however, he will be saved and when he is saved, he will become an honest man we can truly trust, just like all truly born again believers and our revered Apostle Paul. In this regard, please pray for him, as you would pray for any other soul, that he will surrender to Jesus so that Jesus can fully use him for His glory. President Trump will be abandoned and opposed by many of his own friends and political party. In my third book, I outlined when Jeffrey Epstein was arrested, The Lord spoke and said to me the word "blackmail"indicating to me that Jeffrey Epstein was a blackmailer. It came out in all media that he was blackmailing many influential and powerful leaders of the US, foreign Governments, as well as many wealthy influential people worldwide. Many unnamed politicians were caught up in the trap, and now being blackmailed secretly, many of these politicians will be threatened and will turn against President Trump. Mr Trump was a friend of Epstein and might have some dirt come out about him also. Very interesting few months ahead of us. The 'office' of the U.S. Presidency has lost prestige and respect from the American people, the people of foreign countries are reasoning, that if you Americans don't respect the office of your President, why should we respect him or the U.S. President's office, or even your nation either? Respect and American influence has been badly bruised and battered worldwide. The American people have forgotten that when the USA sneezes, the world catches a cold and that if the USA is lost to the globalists, then the world will belong to the globalists to control and implement their satanic new world order, one world Babylon government Agenda. This will then be satan's time to reign on earth through the son of perdition. America must put up one last fight to fight against the globalist Agenda and domination as America is the last standing significant Christian nation. Agenda 21 must not allowed to be the new world order, not right now anyway. America has long ago been infiltrated by traitorous leaders in very high positions, you can sniff them out now during this time of crisis by their policy moves and speech. These sellout satanic globalist puppets are bought and paid for handsomely with large money. Mega billionaires, corporations with global leverage, the secret society satanists have positioned themselves to strike and are sensing their moment now. Fast and pray for President Trump, CODE the scriptures for him and his administration, when you do, God will give a short reprieve for the Christians to get ready to find safe haven, hiding places overseas and away from the USA to protect them from a more intense tribulation time, this is a run to the hills moment. This is the revelation that God has given me.

Look for a furious violent civil warlike outpouring across the USA, along with wars and war skirmishes in a few overseas countries the USA will attack to cover up, draw attention away from the dirt and fallout that's about to be revealed about these big fishes, it's the dialectic at work. Again the deadline for the new world Babylon Agenda must be kept, unless The Lord intervenes with His own AGENDA soon, which He will when we begin to declare His Words. God will dispatch mighty angels to save His chosen and elect.

U.N. AGENDA 21 For Sustainable Development

Noble name and noble sounding agenda of men, omitting Jesus.

This is the reason for the great disturbances in the USA today, and the misery index in the USA will climb higher as we get closer to the November 2020 election and move nearer to January 2021. The end game is to drive President Trump from office as he is not a globalist, but a great US patriot. To cause worldwide consternation, fear, dread by the use of the dialectic, so that the agenda can be brought into full force, satan and the son of perdition must have their moment of fame.

This is the AGENDA and the timeline, the goal of–10 years–to complete it, see for yourself, this is public world information copied from the U.N. website so see for yourself, note the word GLOBAL (whole world):

Taken from the website of the un.org–Decade of Action

The 17 Sustainable Goals are:
No poverty
0 Hunger
Good Health and Well Being
Quality Education

Gender Equality
Clean Water and Sanitation
Affordable and Clean Energy
Decent Work and Economic Growth
Industry, Innovation and Infrastructure
Reduced Inequalities
Sustainable Cities and Communities
Responsible Consumption and production
Climate Action
Life Below Water
Life on Land
Peace Justice and Strong Institutions
Partnerships for the Goals.

Decade of Action
Ten years to transform our world

The <u>Sustainable Development Goals</u> — our shared vision to end poverty, rescue the planet and build a peaceful world — are gaining global momentum.

With just 10 years to go, an ambitious global effort is underway to deliver the 2030 promise—by mobilizing more governments, civil society, businesses and calling on all people to make the Global Goals their own.

Decade of Action to deliver the Global Goals
Today, <u>progress</u> is being made in many places, but, overall, action to meet the Goals is not yet advancing at the speed or scale required. 2020 needs to usher in a decade of ambitious action to deliver the Goals by 2030.

The Decade of Action calls for accelerating sustainable solutions to all the world's biggest challenges — ranging from poverty and gender to climate change, inequality and closing the finance gap.

In September 2019, the UN <u>Secretary-General</u> called on all sectors of society to mobilize for a decade of action on three levels: **global action** to secure greater leadership, more resources and smarter solutions for the Sustainable Development Goals; **local action** embedding the needed transitions in the policies, budgets, institutions and regulatory frameworks of governments, cities and local authorities; and **people action**, *including by youth, civil society, the media, the private sector, unions, academia and other stakeholders, to generate an unstoppable movement pushing for the required transformations.*

***My notes, end of U.N. copied statement.

A TEN YEAR MASTER PLAN TO DELIVER THE NEW WORLD ORDER ULTIMATE BABYLON GLOBAL GOALS.

So the plan is a Ten year master plan engineered to start in 2021, thus; AGENDA 21, to terminate in 2030 when the earth will be under a one world flag and banner. An agenda to bring the whole world to it's knees begging for a way out, a hero deliverer to lead them out, one person with the answers, solution to the mess the world is in, The man needed for the job is Jesus, but that man who the world will clamor for will be satan's seed, the son of perdition. Just as Jesus was rejected by the Jews and Barabbas was angrily and vociferously chosen by the crowd over Jesus.

So the globalists have said a mouthful, let's break it down.

Sustainable Development.
What does it mean?

Sustainable = able to be maintained at a certain rate or level.

It has been spoken many times by the experts in many different areas of expertise that the world as it is cannot sustain the billions of humanity that is in it right now. The world has three times too many people to sustain them. The debt to GDP ratios of many nations are unsustainable. Continuous payouts to support the poor and needy, pensions, medical care are all unsustainable we were told. The end result being that there is a massive need to eliminate the recipients of these financial payouts, in other words, eliminate this 'surplus population' or 'useless eaters'.

This now begs for an answer, a final solution, a plan to be developed to tackle this situation, hence AGENDA 2021 for Sustainable Development.

In true Babylon style, men from 178 nations got together in Rio De Janeiro in 1992 and approved this master plan that has to kickoff in January of 2021 and all oppositions must be silenced, removed they say and believe. BUT Jesus has another plan, and His plan is the prevailing plan. The time is not yet. I believe that for the sake of the Christians, Jesus will put a monkey wrench in the plans and delay it because His people are not aware of it and not prepared either. This is the reason I write to warn the believers and the world of what's going to go down so proper preparations can be made for such a time and we will not be caught, or be taken by surprise. Get ready to run to the hills.

Development = state of developing or being developed:
- a specified state of growth or advancement:
- a new and refined product or idea:
- an event constituting a new stage in a changing situation:

2 the process of starting to experience or suffer from an ailment or feeling

This is the action plan to develop the operational leg of this master plan step by step with it's key components. This is where the dialectic of the Corona virus and the resulting chaos that follows comes in. The idea, is to keep the masses off their feet, unbalanced driven by fear and confusion. This will be the created problem. The misery index will increase greatly in the USA and the world, not because of shortages in many cases, but because of the Agenda, and KARMA, the reaping of what was sown. There will be long lines for foods, gas, to enter buildings, offices, business places, long waits. What was caused by the USA to happen in many nations will come home to the USA. The misery will become unbearable, bribery will be rampant, even in the U.S. Government offices to get things done, just like poorer countries. Fainting, dropping out, quitting will vastly increase, homelessness, drug use and dependency, suicides will be commonplace.

A new chaotic event will occur almost every month, to make the misery index even more unbearable, so the U.S. and world-wide masses will cry out, beg for a solution an answer from the TEN PERCENTERS. The solution will then be offered which the masses will take very quickly so as to get out of the conditions of misery.

A Green New Deal will be Promoted as sustainable by the globalists.

Every thing green and get rid of fossil fuels and everything else right now.

This will be the major thrust of the globalists, do it now and do it quickly will be their demands.

This will be their new developmental areas with warp speed. The 17 goals outlined by them spells this out clearly.

The desired end is the ULTIMATE ONE WORLD BABYLON NEW WORLD ORDER.

Revelation 13 Contemporary English Bible

14This second beast fooled people on earth by working miracles for the first one. Then it talked them into making an idol in the form of the beast that did not die after being wounded by a sword. 15It was allowed to put breath into the idol, so it could speak. Everyone who refused to worship the idol of the beast was put to death. 16 All people were forced to put a mark on their right hand or forehead. Whether they were powerful or weak, rich or poor, free people or slaves, 17they all had to have this mark, or else they could not buy or sell anything. This mark stood for the name of the beast and for the number of its name.

The Reaping Season is here now.

When God's people sinned against Him He sent plagues, or pestilences against them as an affliction to bring them back to Him, so we can see that these rulers are now in the business of playing God to control men on satan's behalf. The Lord will respond to these wicked men, evil globalists by sending His own plagues which will plague them and their children, they will never escape. He will search them out and destroy them.

Whatever men has sown, they shall also reap, national sowing brings national reaping. Personal sowing brings personal reaping, all men will reap whatsoever they have sown, for God is The Lord of the harvest, the righteous paymaster;

Exodus 9:13-15

13 And the Lord said unto Moses, Rise up early in the morning, and stand before Pharaoh, and say unto him, Thus saith the Lord God of the Hebrews, Let my people go, that they may serve me.

14 For I will at this time send all my plagues upon thine heart, and upon thy servants, and upon thy people; that thou mayest know that there is none like me in all the earth.

15 For now I will stretch out my hand, that I may smite thee and thy people with pestilence; and thou shalt be cut off from the earth.

***Satan must telegraph all he is about to do because he imitates God, God reveals His moves by the mouth of His Prophets;

Amos 3:7

7 Surely the Lord God will do nothing, but he revealeth his secret unto his servants the prophets.

The ultimate deception-counterfeit, the "HEAD SHOT" is coming.

The new world order–one world Babylon leader who will imitate Nimrod the first Babylon leader is coming soon as the stage is being set for him now.

The ultimate deception, will be brought upon the world by the hunger of mankind seeking a human savior, a superhero to save them from the distress of nations with perplexity.

Have you ever been deceived, defrauded, caught in a trap? Conned out of money, deceived by a bad husband or wife? By a well known person, one whom you trusted, believed in, thought that you would not be hurt by this person, but something happened to destroy that trust, your bubble burst and your whole world caved in. Then after every thing, you thought it through, the emotions cooled then the realization hits home, I am still here, I am alive and I must pick up the pieces and carry on.

The people of the world under satan's spell, has rejected Jesus Christ as savior and Lord. This master stroke of evil genius, plays upon the number one response of most humans, the *EMOTIONS.* Satan's aim and purpose is; to get powerful emotional human responses and not allow the logic and reason of God's Word to prevail. Satan = explode emotionally now, get depressed later, while with God = come now, let's reason together, let's talk about it, let me solve the problems for you.

The world will be calling a man messiah, anointed one, lord and savior, god, chosen one, world famous, best loved. These are all names or titles that will be given to the coming false messiah, the lawless one, son of perdition. The cry is growing louder and louder and getting stronger and stronger day by day, slowly but surely, the stage is being set for the "**Greatest Deception Show on Earth".**

The cry has already gone out from the masses of humanity, "come and save us someone, anyone, our troubles are relentless and more than we can bear", as they seek a human leader, savior, superhero, god. There is no more reasoning that one can reason with the conditioned masses of people as their hearts are emotionally fixed upon a human person with the right answers. Remember when the angry raucous crowd emotionally shouted,*"Away with Jesus, give us Barrabas"?*

They will do so again. As *Christian futurists,* we are getting ready for the future to be fulfilled. Out of great chaos and confusion, order must come, so the person that presents some cool emotional answers, solutions will be listened to by the masses, followed and worshipped with the chief cheerleader being the false Prophet. Satan the deceiver, troublemaker who is the one causing all the problems in the world, will have an answer, he will hold back his demons from robbing, killing, destroying for a while so the man of sin, the man he indwells can be positioned and installed as a one world ruler. This is satan's shining moment. The world will reject knowledge and acceptance of the only Savior Jesus Christ, whose name alone can save us, but those whose names are written in the Lamb's Book of Life will never worship satan, only Jesus;

Acts 4:12

12 Neither is there salvation in any other: for there is none other name under heaven given among men, whereby we must be saved.

Philippians 2:10-11

10 That at the name of Jesus every knee should bow, of things in heaven, and things in earth, and things under the earth;
11 And that every tongue should confess that Jesus Christ is Lord, to the glory of God the Father.

Already lurking in the shadows of time, is a man, waiting for an opportune moment, he is a deceiver, impostor, counterfeiter who seeks to steal the recognition, worship and adoration from Jesus. This is an age old plan of satan, as I have said before, satan needs a human body to possess, indwell and work through as he is an invisible fallen angel, and can only be in one place at one time. Omnipresence, being every where all at once, an attribute, belongs only to The Lord.

The man of sin, the son of perdition, the lawless one, many call him the anti-Christ, is alive and well, is very well known and loved by billions of people across the world even right now.

This man is a surprisingly astute, narcissistic, egomaniacal politician that has already tasted of and knows the corridors of power but hungers for the ultimate power which is never ever given to men. That power is the power of worship from other humans as god. That power to speak, act like, be god-like and have all people, worship him and be obeyed dutifully, or be killed.

The voices of emotional outrage will drown out the voices of logic and reason, The voices of the tell me what I want to hear crowd, will drown out the voices of let's reason about this crowd. The sane voices will be marginalized or ridiculed, this is the old fashioned playbook that satan uses at all times, drown out truth tellers with thunderous blustering noises, or even eliminate them. Satan did so with many Prophets of God and Jesus, he will play this card again to eliminate all opposition.

Now clearly understand that satan needs a human body to possess and operate from, to speak and do all he desires through. When this man is worshipped and adored by the world, and satan will use great deception to fulfill this, satan will receive that adoration and worship. This man will be like Barabbas, chosen by those who reject Jesus, under satan's deceit. The Word of God says, that man will sit in the temple of God, claiming that he is god and command worship. There is no physical temple of God on earth now that is designated as such, so many people believe that a third temple has to be built in Israel for this to be fulfilled. This will not be of God, but of foolish deceived Israel, men still looking for their messiah.

Look out for these developments to occur very rapidly as Israel draws closer to Saudi Arabia, the guardians of Mecca and the Sunni Sect of Islam. This triad now becomes USA, Israel, and Saudi Arabia the three mono-theistic religions of the world coming together to join their respective religions of Christianity, Islam and Judaism to form a one world church, the false Prophet is now working on this agenda.

Description of the beast (Man) .
* * *Rose up out of the masses (Sea) of people swiftly like a leopard.*
* * *Leopard-like, swift, cunning, spotted, white and black.*
* * *7 Continents, 10 powers (Nations)*
* * *Bear feet-ideological positional standing (communism?).*
* * *Mouth of lion-speaks powerfully, authoritatively roaring* <u>like</u> *a lion, but not the real Lion.*
* * *Given satanic power, position, great authority.*

Revelation 13:0-18

1 And I stood upon the sand of the sea, and saw a beast rise up out of the sea, having seven heads and ten horns, and upon his horns ten crowns, and upon his heads the name of blasphemy.

2 And the beast which I saw was like unto a leopard, and his feet were as the feet of a bear, and his mouth as the mouth of a lion: and the dragon gave him his power, and his seat, and great authority.

A deadly head wound miraculously healed.

3 And I saw one of his heads as it were wounded to death; and his deadly wound was healed: and all the world wondered after the beast.

***The dragon, satan, is invisible and has to indwell someone. So he possesses, indwells this man, called the beast.

So the commendation, adoration, praising of this man, all goes to satan, because satan fully dwells in this man, the beast. This is serious deception, the beast, man is therefore a master deceiver-counterfeiter.

> 4 And they worshipped the dragon which gave power unto the beast: and they worshipped the beast, saying, Who is like unto the beast? who is able to make war with him?

***This man, the beast will speak great blasphemies against God, but God gave him power to continue three and a half years. God measures, limits his days and at the end of his time, God says, *"Time's up, now it's my time"*.

Just as with Job, satan's rope, how far he can go, how long he can continue is measured by God Almighty.

> 5 And there was given unto him a mouth speaking great things and blasphemies; and power was given unto him to continue forty and two months.

> 6 And he opened his mouth in blasphemy against God, to blaspheme his name, and his tabernacle, and them that dwell in heaven.

***This man, the beast will war with the saints of God, he will overpower many of them, because God gave Him that authority, except those who will use *BIBLE CODE 7* strategy, the sworn promises of God. All the world will be under his power. Those whose names are not written in the book of life will worship him. There will be martyrdom of many of the saints, a choice will be given, deny Jesus, worship satan and live, don't deny Jesus, then you die. What will you do?

7 And it was given unto him to make war with the saints, and to overcome them: and power was given him over all kindreds, and tongues, and nations.

8 And all that dwell upon the earth shall worship him, whose names are not written in the book of life of the Lamb slain from the foundation of the world.

9 If any man have an ear, let him hear.

10 He that leadeth into captivity shall go into captivity: he that killeth with the sword must be killed with the sword. Here is the patience and the faith of the saints.

***This beast is another deceiver, a religious man of the church, he has horns like a lamb, he looks like, sounds like, has the manners of a lamb, a Christian leader, Pastor-Shepherd, but he is not, he is a deceiver, counterfeit–bogus, a wolf in sheep's clothing. He opens his mouth to speak and out of the abundance of his heart his mouth speaks blasphemous, heretical demonic things. This false prophet is alive now speaking evil, unscriptural things, he is a satanic agent, also in-dwelt by one of satan's chief demons, as satan can only be in one place or person at a time.

11 And I beheld another beast coming up out of the earth; and he had two horns like a lamb, and he spake as a dragon.

The beast's deadly wound.

The wound of the man-beast was healed, as if miraculously. A scene from a third rate movie will be bought into, hook, line, and sinker by the unsaved world of deceived people. Just like Jesus, who died and rose again on the third day, The ultimate deception-counterfeit will imitate The Lord Jesus's death, burial and resurrection.

> 12 And he exerciseth all the power of the first beast before him, and causeth the earth and them which dwell therein to worship the first beast, whose deadly wound was healed.

***Great tricks that seems like miraculous wonders will be done by this religious man, fire will come down from heaven at his command, he deceives by these tricks.

> 13 And he doeth great wonders, so that he maketh fire come down from heaven on the earth in the sight of men,

The beast wounded by the sword but lived. (John did not know of a gun or bullets.)

The best trick is saved for last, this is an oscar award winning trick from an Oscar Award winning director. As billions of people will be deceived by it and lose their souls by worshipping, sympathizing with this man imitating Jesus's death and resurrection from the dead 3 days later. He was wounded by a sword (Gun) and did live.

*** This is the trigger event, I believe, for all guns and ammo confiscation, bar none, worldwide, so no one can rise up and resist this beast-man. The whole world must be disarmed by force, threats of death by this emotional outrage. The mark or tag of the beast will then be commanded to be placed in the right hand or forehead of all humans, else no buying or selling.

Everything will happen suddenly, great commotion, confusion, guilt, outrage, and a huge backlash will follow.

Think carefully out of the box now, *of what religion and race will the setup accused shooter be?*

Seeing how satan hates Jesus Christ and Christians, you've already gotten the answer to his religion, but of what race will he be?

To think out of the box, one must be privy to what's in the box.

What race of people is being fought against now vehemently? You fill in the blanks.

Demonic emotional order will follow these events. This is the Dialectic. It has already been pre-planned down to the very last details. That's why the Word of God reveals it here in the Bible, it's just a matter of when, the correct timing for this trigger event to unfold. The moment is soon to come.

The false prophet will then command worship of this deceiver, proclaiming, "Who is like him?".

The mark of the beast will be demanded to be had in the right hand or in the forehead to either buy or sell, for all humans rich or poor, free or bondservants. Country folks off grid will be ok, but not city folks, or on grid folks.

14 And deceiveth them that dwell on the earth by the means of those miracles which he had power to do in the sight of the beast; saying to them that dwell on the earth, that they should make an image to the beast, which had the wound by a sword, and did live.

15 And he had power to give life unto the image of the beast, that the image of the beast should both speak, and cause that as many as would not worship the image of the beast should be killed.

16 And he causeth all, both small and great, rich and poor, free and bond, to receive a mark in their right hand, or in their foreheads:

17 And that no man might buy or sell, save he that had the mark, or the name of the beast, or the number of his name.

18 Here is wisdom. Let him that hath understanding count the number of the beast: for it is the number of a man; and his number is Six hundred threescore and six.

***Satan has already made his intentions known that he will be like the most high and will be worshipped as god, to do so he will use mass deception on a very grand scale to deceive the very gullible masses who are already primed and pumped for such deception. Satan already has an hierarchy of worshippers, witches, warlocks, secret societies of all evil people who are now deceived and ignorantly giving him honor and he will expand upon these to the ultimate degree, by threats of forced worship or death.

Remember, it's all about **WORSHIPPING THE BEAST-MAN.**

Isaiah 14:13-14

13 For thou hast said in thine heart, I will ascend into heaven, I will exalt my throne above the stars of God: I will sit also upon the mount of the congregation, in the sides of the north:

14 I will ascend above the heights of the clouds; I will be like the most High.

BE WARNED…Recap—

A made up occurrence of a shot to the head of a very well known popular, worldwide admired man that will be passed off as real, "The HEAD SHOT, HEAD WOUND is coming."
There will be a man in the very near future, a very popular, well liked man, a favorite of the whole world, so much so that when he was first introduced to the international world's scene, he created a sensational buzz among all peoples of the world. He will join with a great movie director to pull this off.

Everyone knows his name, well, he's coming back on the world's scene as the one who will be shot in the head, wounded to death by a terrible head wound, but after three days he miraculously shows himself to be alive and well. The whole world will marvel, because the expert doctors and medical personnel who will be in on this charade, will attest to his deadly wound being real, as well as the fact that he was **PRONOUNCED DEAD**. The cameras will pan constantly upon that scene of the **HEADSHOT**, and pan over and over, riveting this audio visual replay loud and long, billions of people worldwide will see it and be deceived into believing it. Tell a big lie long enough and loud enough, billions will believe it. The cameras that will have caught these scenes will belong to many different news organizations. The reporters on scene will report in furious haste and in urgent fashion what has happened, not realizing that, this was a *SETUP, a well outlined scripted plan of deception. Great mourning, indignation, lamentation will follow for two full days.*

On the third day, it will be miraculously announced that he is alive and well, he will show himself off, as being very well, and alive and uninjured, and begin to receive waves of accolades and worship. Who is as great as the beast (This man, counterfeit)? they will ask in admiration, not knowing it is gross deception.

The beast will then be proclaimed as the messiah, the christ, the anointed one by the false prophet. All those still seeking the messiah like the Jewish people will be deceived by him. All persons will be forced to worship him as god, except the Jesus people. He will become world President, ruling the whole world. The beast's second coming will be heralded around the whole world.

This is the man, the deceiver-counterfeiter that has come to fulfill the call, the desperate desire from the wicked world for their savior after rejecting *THE ONLY TRUE AND LIVING SAVIOR JESUS CHRIST.*

This deceiver-counterfeiter will now swallow up the whole world of non-Christians, those whose names are not written in the Lamb's Book of Life, in total deception, bar none, and has now become; a man savior, a man god and now man worship is fully commenced across the nations of the world and given to him in Babylon style worship.

An order will soon go out from the religious false prophet with an arm of military and police enforcement to kill all persons who do not worship this man or his image, his holographic facsimile or recite / say his creed acknowledging him as god, as he can only be in one place at a time. (He does not possess like Jesus; Omnipresence). Martial law will be in all the nations, as all are forced to worship this lawless man of sin, possessed by satan himself and pretending to be God.

It is vitally important that we understand the word *IMAGE*. Image does not mean a picture, reflection only, but look carefully at these definitions of the word.

Image = reflection or likeness, representation of physical or mental.

copy or emblem, rhetorical speech.
* A creed or statement of belief or allegiance that is verbally recited.

A recital of a creed, a confession with the mouth and belief in the heart. In Christianity acceptance of Jesus is declared–verbalized, one's faith in Jesus Christ is declared. We now are conformed to the image of Jesus upon doing so in faith.

This man and his cohorts resorts to murder of his opponents, he tolerates no opposition. Violence follows ignorance very closely. No reasoning or dialogue is allowed at all, it's obey and worship or die. Satan always seek to imitate or counterfeit Jesus Christ in every way, and to achieve his wicked agenda and deceive even the very elect if possible this is his strategy. In like manner as Jesus Christ was crucified and then laid down his life, three days was he in the grave but rose from the dead triumphantly on the third day. Jesus is *ALIVE* and seated at the right hand of God now. So will the deceiver-counterfeiter fake his own death for three days and then announce himself miraculously well in a death-defying movie scripted deception setup.

BE WARNED, DON'T BE DECEIVED, THIS HEAD SHOT IS FAKE!
IT'S A SETUP TO DECEIVE THE GULLIBLE MASSES OF THE WORLD!

The ultimate *SIMON SAYS* is about to unfold and the *"man of sin"* will have the people whose names are not written in the Book of Life eating out of his hands. This man will become power drunk and power mad, ballistically delusional, narcissistic, brutally wicked and murderous as satan grips him even tighter. Satan, this created being of eternity that is locked into time, knows the clock is ticking and his time short. The master of death and hell will unleash death and bloodshed all over the world as he robs, kills, and destroys.

He will make Adolph Hitler look like an innocent choir boy.

Let's get and retain Biblical information and revelation and begin to pray and plead the blood of Jesus earnestly against the ***IMAGINATIONS OF THE THOUGHTS*** of these wicked individuals as all this evil will be occurring there in the heart of men. Let's make our calling and election sure, no one can predict the future as to how or when they will die, so let us fight as much as we can not to be a victim of this man, but for a way of escape so we can go up in the catching away when Jesus returns. We will be the massive group that have come through great tribulation. (Revelation7;13-14)

***This is one vision of my Assistant Pastor Stacy McDonald, a great Preacher-Teacher-Prophetess of God whose books will be forthcoming shortly. A woman of God to whom God has given many visions of national and world leaders conversations and actions.

I am in this place and there is this young guy sitting at this table in what felt like a restaurant. It was breakfast time and he was sitting at this table, but he did not want me to recognize him. He was trying very hard for me not to recognize him, but people were shouting for him and celebrating him. He was a political leader, a world leader of some sort. The people loved his policies and what he stood for. The were hailing him for being charismatic and suave and for just being a "plain likeable guy." A people person and a lot of the things he had presented echoed well with the people. (The weird thing was the person that I saw in front of me was an actor I saw in a show.

U.N. Agenda 2021, The New World Order, 'Ultimate One World Babylon'.

In the show I saw this actor in, his character in the show was a tech savvy guy who was a hacker and very much onto bitcoins.)

He rises from the table and rises up literally like he is being lifted and as he rises up, he is in the middle of this square a public place. He bodily rises up and turns in to a statue much like or similar to how the Paul Revere statue is, that same type of material. As he turns into this statue I hear "the nuclear weapon has been deployed. At this very moment war planes began to fly. The people began to run and scream and there was such chaos in the atmosphere. I said to the people "This is what you wanted, this is what you asked for," and they began wailing "This is not what he said he would do."

So, I looked over and said to the angel that was taking me around in this vision "oh so it is like they were double crossed," and the voice said "yes they were double crossed."

I felt like I was up in the air and then I felt as though I was somewhere on the international spectrum. I heard the name of a country, but I could not remember the name of the country when I awakened. As I was airborne it felt like an atmosphere of war it felt like war planes were about. This was the end of the vision.

INTERPRETATION

The second half of the vision:

There is a world leader that is going to rise to power on the international stage. He is going to be charismatic, suave, and well liked by many. The things he will present will appeal to the masses and they will celebrate and revere him and support his policies. He will tell the people what they like to hear, but in his rise to power he will do the complete opposite of what they expected him to do and he will cause 2 things the deployment of some type of a nuclear weapon and the unleashing of a cyber attack. What he will do will have a very strong effect on the international community and will unleash war. The people will be in shock and regret because their leader would have deceived, and double crossed them because they would get the total opposite of whom they thought they were getting.

Him rising from the chair signifies his rise to power and his position being solidified set in stone. ***End of Vision.

GOING THROUGH GREAT TRIBULATION.
Do not fear believers, we are untouchables, through BIBLE CODE 7, God's Force-Power 4 change.

Let the believers understand that as all this is unfolding, a jealous God will be rendering judgements, thunderings from above, yes He will be. He will terrify the whole earth of satan worshippers while His worshippers will be kept in perfect peace as our minds are stayed, fixed upon Him. His angels will keep us in all our ways, we the elect, are untouchables, unstoppable all through this great tribulation period. The days will be shortened for our sakes, all deceptions aimed at us will be worthlessly ineffective. Jesus will be a shield about us and the lifter of our heads.

<u>New Living Translation</u>
<u>2 Thessalonians 2</u>
Events prior to the Lord's Second Coming.

1Now, dear brothers and sisters,*ᵃ* let us clarify some things about the coming of our Lord Jesus Christ and how we will be gathered to meet him. 2Don't be so easily shaken or alarmed by those who say that the day of the Lord has already begun. Don't believe them, even if they claim to have had a spiritual vision, a revelation, or a letter supposedly from us.

A clear warning about deception from so called believers. Foolish believers like the foolish virgins will believe many things they see and hear and seek to convince the wise believers to do the same, but remember, wise virgins will never be convinced by foolish virgin's deceptions. A great division in the Church is coming between wise and foolish virgins the real believers and those who are easily deceived and led astray. So this rebellion against God, and falling away, will surely come first.

2 Thessalonians 2

3Don't be fooled by what they say. For that day will not come until there is a great rebellion against God and the man of lawlessness*b* is revealed—the one who brings destruction.*c* 4He will exalt himself and defy everything that people call god and every object of worship. He will even sit in the temple of God, claiming that he himself is God.

5Don't you remember that I told you about all this when I was with you? 6And you know what is holding him back, for he can be revealed only when his time comes. 7For this lawlessness is already at work secretly, and it will remain secret until the one who is holding it back steps out of the way. 8Then the man of lawlessness will be revealed, but the Lord Jesus will kill him with the breath of his mouth and destroy him by the splendor of his coming.

***Please note carefully that his powers, signs, miracles are all counterfeit, bogus, every evil deception will be used by this man of lawlessness. This man of perdition will do the works of satan with counterfeit power, signs, wonders using every evil deceptions.

9This man will come to do the work of Satan with counterfeit power and signs and miracles. 10He will use every kind of evil deception to fool those on their way to destruction, because they refuse to love and accept the truth that would save them. 11So God will cause them to be greatly deceived, and they will believe these lies. 12Then they will be condemned for enjoying evil rather than believing the truth.

Wise believers should Stand Firm, with no fear.

As you have already hidden and secured yourself in the vault of God through *BIBLE CODE 7*, now as you consistently declare His Word, His angels will keep and preserve you from all evil and remember that The Lord will shorten the days for His chosen ones sakes.

This is the coded scripture, the sworn promise that God has given to us of not only our salvation, but that we will not die, but press forward boldly, confidently through *the great tribulation untouched*, but purified like fine silver tested 7 times in the fire through the self defense, self preservation strategy of *BIBLE CODE 7.*

Other Books By Dr. Norman Dacosta

Chapter 4

When Men Say Peace And Safety, A Titanic Moment Is About To Happen.

How does one prepare for an unknown Titanic future? Physically? Spiritually?

GOD"S SOLUTION, AND GOD"S WAY TO ENDURE–FOR THIS TRIBULATION SEASON–BIBLE CODE 7.
The strategy that gives the ability to go upstream in a downstream world.

The staying power strategy of, endurance, being wired to win.

BIBLE CODE 7 The minesweeping strategy of destroying satan's land mines from your path.

BIBLE CODE 7 The only security option.

BIBLE CODE 7 The Spiritual Nuclear option for the Jesus Believers.

BIBLE CODE 7 Your Samson Option

BIBLE CODE 7 Your Self preservation manual

BIBLE CODE 7 Your Self defense manual

BIBLE CODE 7 Your Conflict resolution strategy
BIBLE CODE 7 Your Crisis management strategy
BIBLE CODE 7 Your Takedown, achilles heel and body destroyer for your enemies, secret or open.

Jesus did not die to help us to cope, Jesus died to help us to conquer, wreck, destroy the works of the devil.

Through BIBLE CODE 7, God Himself will chop and dice your adversaries in little pieces, the battle is not yours.

It is very important to know and understand that the spiritual DNA that comes down to every person helps to determine who and what they are, what they will become and also what they will accomplish in life.

That the spiritual DNA from your ancestors may break, bring defeat, failure, misery, or success to come and a good warfare must be waged against this demonic force trying to keep one in bondage and servitude as in the days of slavery. What was molded into the slaves by the slave masters and owners comes down the generational lines. What was molded into the slave owners and masters also came down their generational lines, that's why they desire to rule and control, harass and oppress the masses of the people now in the same manner as of the bygone past because those demons of oppression and control does not die but continues their assignments from generation to generation. The rich ruling over the poor.

When the music dancing, singing and shouting is over then what?

With what is the onslaught of hell and satan's demons handled?

With what is the devil countered to make him heel and kneel in obedience to your will and desires?

How does one turn back sicknesses, diseases, children gone astray, gale force winds of misfortune in one's life?

Can generational curses and misfortunes be destroyed? When everything seems to go wrong, is there a way to make it go right?

Is there a way to make satan get behind you and not be a stumbling block before you?

Who will war and fight for you when you can't fight for yourself?

The answers to all these questions I am uniquely qualified to give as, this is not someone's testimony I am giving, but my own, as I have endured and gone through a near death, living hell experience, but came out valiantly through the self preservation and defense strategy of **BIBLE CODE 7, declaring, reciting the Word of God only 7 Times morning and 7 Times nights. (I started with Psalm 91)**

BIBLE CODE 7 is your assignment to tell, to declare last rites to satan and his demons, they must turn you loose by the speaking, reciting of God's Word 7 Times to power.

BIBLE CODE 7 is a testimony of my personal life and the nightmarish hell and near death experience I endured and overcame with Jesus's help.

It's a self defense and preservation manual to make sure you win and not lose, be a victor and not a victim, live and not die giving Jesus the glory, and living the long prosperous life He promised you.

BIBLE CODE 7 is my Samson option that makes me spiritually un-touchable, it's not an agenda of man but of Jesus Christ. The going again 7 Times declaring the Word of God to effect powerful supernatural results.

BIBLE CODE 7 is a powerful, volcanic revolution and catalytic strategy God revealed to me to be used against all the forces of darkness, to lay hold on to His sworn promises, the Hundredfold, unlock hidden secrets, pull the future into our present so we can prosper and be in great health.

BIBLE CODE 7 is the weaponization of the Word of God to fulfill God's sworn promise, "The battle is not yours, but the Lord's." God's Word will be performed by Him.

BIBLE CODE 7 is the master key strategy of God to take by force and keep God's sworn promises of hundredfold health, prosperity and great success.

BIBLE CODE 7 is a spiritual security and alarm system for your spirit, mind, body, home, family and possessions.

BIBLE CODE 7 is the master key strategy of God to break the hold of hell off your life yourself, by fasting and the Word of God, as many Bishops, Pastors are not equipped to cast out devils by experience or anointing.

BIBLE CODE 7 weaponizes the Word of God only to forcefully move the 800 pound spiritual gorilla in the room, they must move by the authority of God's Word, the 'it is written'.

BIBLE CODE 7 is a strategy of taking the gloves off and going to extreme warfare against anti-Jesus bigotry and the destruction of satanic works.

BIBLE CODE 7 used constantly develops nerves of steel, ferocity of lions and eyes of eagles in the user as one sees powerful results time after time.

BIBLE CODE 7 must be backed up by fasting to work, Jesus said so.

BIBLE CODE 7 is the God revealed strategy of dealing with all enemies, seen and unseen, known and unknown, shattering the hidden hand of satan from off your life, children's lives and all your affairs by decreeing His Words only.

BIBLE CODE is the strategy to be used to penetrate new territory, bring destruction and devastation, to shatter, pillage and burn the unfruitful works of darkness. To bring abundant supply where there is lack, order out of chaos, light where there is darkness, good where there is evil and vibrant health where there is sickness, to make normal what is or has become abnormal.

BIBLE CODE 7, speaking the Word only, is a revolution whose time has come that will shatter your conditioning, change your responses, brighten your outlook, mold your thoughts to that of a victor and not of a victim.

BIBLE CODE 7 will change your speech pattern from speaking death, to the declaration of life and abundant sworn blessings, His Words, that was promised from God Almighty.

BIBLE CODE 7 will shatter the technological enslavement that is occurring now upon the masses of people by the use of multiple technological devices and their tracking features and bring them under the dominion authority of Jesus Christ.

BIBLE CODE 7 is the reset strategy needed to shatter, reset, reprogram the satanic conditioning that has been implanted in the heart for many years and give the refreshing victory The Lord has intended for those who surrender to Him.

BIBLE CODE 7 is the elimination and total destruction of the strange foreign fires of contaminated worship from the emotions that has been offered as worship upon the altars before Him, and to bring back the true and only fire, the Word of God, to worship Him so He can confirm His Word only with the signs following. He is a Spirit and must be worshipped in Spirit and in Truth.

BIBLE CODE 7 is the 7 fold, (7 times) recital, declaration of God's Word only over your situation or conditions in life whether sicknesses, poverty, lack, problems at home, demonic oppression, demonic possession. No demon of hell can stand in your way, no stumbling block of hell can stop you, no witch or warlock can oppose you. Satan must erase your name from his book of bad luck. It's time to come out of your grinding poverty, depression, sickness, hopelessness, helplessness and despair. The powerful vibration patterns of God's Words will shatter and destroy all evil in and around you.

Whenever and wherever anyone or an attorney goes before a Judge, they present their case and backs up their presentations by the written Law, with sections, paragraphs etc. The Judge is therefore constrained by "The Law, what is written", and must make a ruling based upon the written law.

So it is with God, He only responds to His Word, 'the it is written of God', the Bible, declared from your lips. When we begin to use *BIBLE CODE 7*, to recite, declare His Words, God is now constrained, obligated to perform His Word on behalf of His Lambs. Why? It is His sworn promise to His children.

Titanic moments are here...suddenly, unannounced!

Thousands of financially secure, retired, pensioned money spending seniors with disposable incomes who patronize restaurants, go on cruises, travel and shop are succumbing to Covid 19, or are self quarantining for safety. So billions of dollars are lost or not being spent from this financially secure segment of the population worldwide. As long as Covid is threatening, the world's economies are threatened. Hundreds of thousands of businesses large and small are shuttering for good as Covid round two comes into focus. Schools and Universities are still uncertain of reopening this coming fall. While all this is happening, eleven million people are facing evictions from rental properties, and mortgages are going unpaid in the USA. Homelessness is increasing and hope for many is fading fast.

The banks are losing trillions of dollars now, and because of these loan losses they will suffer greatly from the Covid 19 shutdowns. No one has to be a rocket scientist to know that as a result of the shutdowns worldwide in every sector of society, the repercussions will be dire, ominous and catastrophic. The reported U.S GDP losses are off the charts at 32.9% (marketwatch.com, July 30,2020).

Here are some of the things that will happen worldwide in our intertwined world as a result of this shutdown (Worldwide catastrophe all at one as never seen before, this is how we know that we are in the great tribulation);

WORLDWIDE there will be:-
1—Massive unemployment.
2—Small and large business bankruptcies.
3—Economic collapse.
4—Banking and Industry Collapse, financial chaos.

5—Societal Breakdown and Collapse, poverty, sicknesses and more diseases.

6—Wars, Shortages, High Inflationary Prices, worthless currencies.

As a result of these, all these things will follow in a domino effect. Failed infrastructure, power grid, telecommunications, water supplies. Total collapse of the rule of law, anarchy, chaos, warlords territorial rule. Financial collapse, followed by an explosion of worldwide riots, burnings. Executions, murders and kidnappings. Political anarchy, attempted revolutions, assassinations of key leaders worldwide

The rise of private security contractors to protect the wealthy and businesses with armed, military-trained guards. A worsening of drug and substance abuse and suicides Increases in child trafficking, child kidnappings for the trafficking trade $. Censorship of all disseminated information including private websites. An explosion in homelessness and tent cities as destitution and despair spreads across the nations. An explosion of squalor, slums, diseases among the close living, moving populations.

Death of millions from, starvation, diseases, drugs, murders despair. The twenty one judgements from God will begin to come upon the world. The ten percenters have already stashed away their monies, in gold and silver, not paper currencies as paper is worthless. For such a time as this that they have created, but God has a real surprise for them, look;

James 5
New Living Translation
Warning to the Rich

1Look here, you rich people: Weep and groan with anguish because of all the terrible troubles ahead of you. 2Your wealth is rotting away, and your fine clothes are moth-eaten rags. 3Your gold and silver are corroded. The very wealth you were counting on will eat away your flesh like fire. This corroded treasure you have hoarded will testify against you on the day of judgment. 4For listen! Hear the cries of the field workers whom you have cheated of their pay. The cries of those who harvest your fields have reached the ears of the LORD of Heaven's Armies.

5You have spent your years on earth in luxury, satisfying your every desire. You have fattened yourselves for the day of slaughter. 6You have condemned and killed innocent people,*a* who do not resist you.*b*

In man's lust for power, they lust for full spectrum dominance. Just like showing all colors and spectrum of the rainbow, in every detail. This has been Babylon USA's plan and strategy over the nations of the world to dominate every aspect of a nation's life and living. To accomplish such dominance bribe money has been lavished around upon these nation's leaders to buy their obedience and control, to get it and maintain it, accompanied by threats and intimidations to toe the USA's line, or else.

The biblical typology is Simon the sorcerer operating from the city of Samaria.

Unknown to both Simon and the USA is that they both possess an achilles heel, a master switch that will destroy them on a moments notice. Whenever an unstoppable force meets an immovable object, something has to give. Jesus is the unstoppable force, the Solid Rock, that meets satan who refuses to give in, end result, his works must be shattered in pieces, for of Jesus's Kingdom there shall be no end. The preaching, proclaiming of Jesus's name and Word destroys all mankind's and satan's schemes and plans.

They must be destroyed, nothing can resist the Word of God, nothing can stand in it's way, every knee must bow to it, all must fall down before it to succumb and worship. The Word is Jesus himself.

Isaiah 13

1 The burden of Babylon, which Isaiah the son of Amoz did see.

2 Lift ye up a banner upon the high mountain, exalt the voice unto them, shake the hand, that they may go into the gates of the nobles.

3 I have commanded my sanctified ones, I have also called my mighty ones for mine anger, even them that rejoice in my highness.

4 The noise of a multitude in the mountains, like as of a great people; a tumultuous noise of the kingdoms of nations gathered together: the Lord of hosts mustereth the host of the battle.

5 They come from a far country, from the end of heaven, even the Lord, and the weapons of his indignation, to destroy the whole land.

***God's weapons of fury to destroy the Babylonian empire, the USA. Old Babylon of Nebuchadnezzar is gone, finished, God is the God of the active alive and living, this is the references to today's world and the USA.

6 Howl ye; for the day of the Lord is at hand; it shall come as a destruction from the Almighty.

7 Therefore shall all hands be faint, and every man's heart shall melt:

8 And they shall be afraid: pangs and sorrows shall take hold of them; they shall be in pain as a woman that travaileth: they shall be amazed one at another; their faces shall be as flames.

9 Behold, the day of the Lord cometh, cruel both with wrath and fierce anger, to lay the land desolate: and he shall destroy the sinners thereof out of it.

10 For the stars of heaven and the constellations thereof shall not give their light: the sun shall be darkened in his going forth, and the moon shall not cause her light to shine.

11 And I will punish the world for their evil, and the wicked for their iniquity; and I will cause the arrogancy of the proud to cease, and will lay low the haughtiness of the terrible.

***The Day of The Lord, a day of dread, fury, fright, judgement a horrible day coming upon the earth to destroy the proud and arrogant from the face of the earth.

12 I will make a man more precious than fine gold; even a man than the golden wedge of Ophir.

13 Therefore I will shake the heavens, and the earth shall remove out of her place, in the wrath of the Lord of hosts, and in the day of his fierce anger.

14 And it shall be as the chased roe, and as a sheep that no man taketh up: they shall every man turn to his own people, and flee every one into his own land.

15 Every one that is found shall be thrust through; and every one that is joined unto them shall fall by the sword.

16 Their children also shall be dashed to pieces before their eyes; their houses shall be spoiled, and their wives ravished.

***The promise to return to Babylon what they have done to others, KARMA, sowing and reaping.

17 Behold, I will stir up the Medes against them, which shall not regard silver; and as for gold, they shall not delight in it.

***The Medes again, God's chosen instruments will come up against invincible Babylon USA to destroy it. No amount of gold or silver will stop them. No amount of modern weaponry, sophisticated technological devices shall matter, it must be destroyed.

18 Their bows also shall dash the young men to pieces; and they shall have no pity on the fruit of the womb; their eye shall not spare children.

19 And Babylon, the glory of kingdoms, the beauty of the Chaldees' excellency, shall be as when God overthrew Sodom and Gomorrah.

***God gives the real reason here for Babylon USA's destruction, as, in the same manner as Sodom and Gomorrah, meaning that they became like these destroyed cities in practices and will receive that same payback paycheck, be made totally waste and desolate, never to be inhabited by humans again.

20 It shall never be inhabited, neither shall it be dwelt in from generation to generation: neither shall the Arabian pitch tent there; neither shall the shepherds make their fold there.

21 But wild beasts of the desert shall lie there; and their houses shall be full of doleful creatures; and owls shall dwell there, and satyrs shall dance there.

22 And the wild beasts of the islands shall cry in their desolate houses, and dragons in their pleasant palaces: and her time is near to come, and her days shall not be prolonged.

This is another prophecy given by the Psalmist of the captives of Babylon as they were taken to Babylon in the captivity in 485 B.C., their lament, their oath of loyalty, and their prophecy, decree of karma, reaping what was sown. As they have done to us, do so unto them Lord. Even thought his prophecy was made to babylon five, it has great prophetic meanings to Babylon six, the USA, as they have invaded and done the same to many nations in making them submit to their rule.

Psalm 137

1 By the rivers of Babylon, there we sat down, yea, we wept, when we remembered Zion.

2 We hanged our harps upon the willows in the midst thereof.

3 For there they that carried us away captive required of us a song; and they that wasted us required of us mirth, saying, Sing us one of the songs of Zion.

4 How shall we sing the Lord's song in a strange land?

5 If I forget thee, O Jerusalem, let my right hand forget her cunning.

6 If I do not remember thee, let my tongue cleave to the roof of my mouth; if I prefer not Jerusalem above my chief joy.

7 Remember, O Lord, the children of Edom in the day of Jerusalem; who said, Rase it, rase it, even to the foundation thereof.

8 O daughter of Babylon, who art to be destroyed; happy shall he be, that rewardeth thee as thou hast served us.

9 Happy shall he be, that taketh and dasheth thy little ones against the stones.

***An awesome prophecy of payback, sowing and reaping, KARMA. What was sown, let them also reap. Praying to The Lord for **His** vengeance upon your enemies is just and right, vengeance belongs to Him alone, so don't seek your own vengeance. Praying for payback is a right and holy act, it is the Word of God;

Galatians 6

7You cannot fool God, so don't make a fool of yourself! You will harvest what you plant. 8If you follow your selfish desires, you will harvest destruction, but if you follow the Spirit, you will harvest eternal life. 9Don't get tired of helping others. You will be rewarded when the time is right, if you don't give up. 10We should help people whenever we can, especially if they are followers of the Lord.

Spiritual warfare mandates that you go ahead, pray for God's vengeance upon the wicked and deceitful that have spoken against you and the Church of Jesus Christ. With all God's richest blessings, but never take vengeance in your own hands. Condemn every enemy tongue speaking against you. The Lord will vindicate you. The enemies encircle you like bees, but in the name of The Lord, my resolution of will is not to be a victim, or loser and be destroyed, but to destroy them utterly. I shall live and not die, I will declare the works of The Lord in the land of the living. God will satisfy me with long life and show me His salvation, I refuse to die an early death, so I will take care of my body and war a good warfare.

Pray for those marked and destined for salvation that they will surrender to Jesus now before it is too late. See here again;

Is. 54 NAS Bible

17"No weapon that is formed against you will prosper;
And every tongue that accuses you in judgment you will condemn.
This is the heritage of the servants of the LORD,
And their vindication is from Me," declares the LORD.

You do the condemnation and allow the Righteous Judge to have His way. This is your gift from The Lord and you are very righteous in doing so.

Chapter 5

Bible Prophecied Destruction Of Babylon Usa.

Escaping Babylon USA through BIBLE CODE 7.

A major power has entered upon the scene in America and an invasion of it has begun by stealth and is terrorizing the masses. So great is that invisible power that almost all of America has responded, succumbed to it, and is being controlled by it with new rules and regulations. It has no bullets, chains or whips, but drives millions into a frenzy, terrorized like a stampeding herd. The frightened, terrified masses are pitted one against the other to battle and devour one another. What is that great weaponry used to do this? The demons of FEAR and CONFUSION!

God's Word declares that God did not give His people that spirit, but one of power, love and a sound mind. Yes, the globalist manipulators has gotten control of the USA and has it where they desire it to be, in their manipulative control utilizing the mass media who find great delight in driving the Covid virus like a whip and a wedge used to scourge the masses into deeper fear and confusion, giving insufficient confusing and misleading bytes of information that drives a wedge of division between the people. Saturation screaming headlines are rampant with a battle of the media giants to see which can scream the loudest. This behavior modification strategy used in America was borrowed from China's playbook, management by crisis, however God has a response to all the actions of men that goes against His plans and agenda. I have written before that God still controls floods, hail, volcanoes, hurricanes, tornadoes, flies, frogs, gnats, locusts, wasps, hornets, all insects and what we call 'acts of God', He still controls all the world and men in it. He rules by His power and men must succumb to His rulership. China has begun a great persecution of the Church of Jesus Christ, God has already responded and will very soon will respond more muscularly with these acts. America has begun to do the same and God will respond likewise.

I believe the American Christians are waking up however, and are beginning to pray. God has heard and is responding to the cry of His people.

The last straw…USA Supreme Court's message to the Church of Jesus Christ- "You are non essential!", Your First Amendment Rights are gone.

The Supreme Court, the head of the USA Courts, has ruled against Jesus Christ, and against the Churches again. The recent ruling from the Supreme Court of the USA regarding Churches is they are non essential businesses, as they have upheld the ruling of the Nevada Courts. In essence, the casinos are essential, they can be opened and have 50% capacity during Covid 19 lockdowns, but the Churches can have maximum 50 people, even if capacity is 1,000, they are seen as not essential.

(Source; The Hill, 7/24/2020; Supreme Court Again rejects Church challenge to virus restrictions) by 5-4 ruling. This lawsuit was about unfair treatment compared to casinos, restaurants, amusement parks in the State of Nevada where the Churches cap is 50 persons maximum per service, even if their building capacity is 1,000. Other businesses were told to cut availability to half 50% of their fire code capacity.

"The U.S. Constitution guarantees, the free exercise of religion, not craps, blackjack or other casino games, but the Governor of Nevada has different priorities", Justice Alito wrote in dissent. It passed anyhow, 5-4 against the Church of Jesus Christ. The 'free exercise of religion' has now been shattered, destroyed by the State of Nevada and the USA, by this Supreme Court ruling.

The first Amendment: An Overview (Cornell Law School)

The First Amendment of the United States Constitution protects the right to freedom of religion and freedom of expression from government interference. It prohibits any laws that establish a national religion, impede the free exercise of religion, abridge the freedom of speech, infringe upon the freedom of the press, interfere with the right to peaceably assemble, or prohibit citizens from petitioning for a governmental redress of grievances. It was adopted into the Bill of Rights in 1791.

This Supreme Court ruling follows the legalization of sodomy in 2016, and Instituting of a National Memorial to homosexual rights, Stonewall, the legalization of abortions, prayers cast out the Schools 1962 and many other abominations.

The **"Assembly of the Wicked"** has enclosed, surrounded Jesus's Church, but they will be destroyed, shattered to pieces;

Psalm 22:16

16 For dogs have compassed me: the assembly of the wicked have inclosed me: they pierced my hands and my feet.

The First Amendment has now been abolished in the USA by this ruling.

But we ought to obey God, not men. No Federal or State Government has ecclesiastical authority over the Churches of Jesus Christ. Jesus Christ only has that authority over His Churches. They have thereby stepped into Jesus's shoes.

Wake up now Christians, persecution of the Churches of Jesus Christ has now been set in the roots, foundations of the State of Nevada and the USA against Jesus by the Supreme Courts. So Nevada and America has now started a war with Jesus Christ. Watch Nevada and the USA receive fiery Judgements from God. A fury is rising in both God and His saints.

A Church resistance is afoot, the Church must either resist or succumb.

The great reset has now begun in earnest and the Church must now arise to warfare by praying without ceasing. God's mercy and restraint to judgement will prevail because of our prayers.

The freedom loving democratic USA silences dissenting voices, shatters their First Amendment rights.

The main crisis worldwide is that there is a war between autocracy vs. democracy. Most of the major powers outside of the USA are autocratic in leadership model, but the USA is a democracy. The USA is rapidly losing it's democratic nature however, and becoming autocratic just like Russia or China. The autocracy begins with the corporate big tech companies and the billionaire ruling class elites. The Government must reign in these monopolistic tech giants and other corporations of a too big to fail nature. The USA's Government leaders and people must return to Jesus Christ to maintain it's democracy, not by a revival as usual, but a minesweeping revolution of a new strategy of self preservation and defense, BIBLE CODE 7, to overcome and survive the scourges of this day and time.

The USA was a nation founded on freedom from religious persecution, or freedom to worship The Lord, but now the worshipping people and Churches has been targeted and designated non essential by the USA Supreme Court and State of Nevada and their right of worship infringed upon. Thank God He does not move in haste for the benefit of His people, but will be patient in judgement for their sakes.

The big technology, big corporate media firms deletes videos, social media accounts, maligns, berates truth tellers to keep the main globalist narratives unchallenged, with no dissent. The messengers of truth are being discredited and maligned, however the messages are reaching home. A cry of censorship is unheeded in the USA, and opposing viewpoints, dissenting opinions are shut down and drowned out, deleted from the internet, websites are taken down by tech giants and people ridiculed immediately by billionaire messiahs. Anyone of the masses are viewed as the permanent underclass to be ruled over by the rich, economic elite, ruling class and globalists. A confrontation between darkness and light is in full blown warfare. The satanic globalists will not tolerate anything, or any voices that they satanically oppose. Is this autocratic Russia or China? No, it's the democratic USA 2020 rapidly losing more of it's democracy, copying the practices of autocratic Socialist Russia and Communist China. Does this sound familiar biblically? Of course, look here;

Acts 4:17-18

17 But that it spread no further among the people, let us straitly threaten them, that they speak henceforth to no man in this name.

18 And they called them, and commanded them not to speak at all nor teach in the name of Jesus.

Videos are banned and removed from the demonic controlled big tech internet platforms, but God will respond, these platforms will begin to crash and burn, and unstoppable other platforms will be raised up anew. Just as they could not stop the spread of the gospel, so will they never stop the dissenting voices. The first ten Amendments in the U.S. Constitution are the Bill of Rights, how long will it be before the other nine are denied to the American people? Not very long if no fight is put up. How can one dissent and stay alive? through BIBLE CODE 7.

Never forget, when an unstoppable force meets an immovable object, something has to give, Jesus Christ is that unstoppable force and all that seems immovable will be shattered, destroyed before Him.

It is much easier to run a society through the dialectic, management by crisis, mental control than through physical control, this is done through confusion, constant misinformation and fear.

The numerous, overburdening laws, rules, regulations, oppressions of the poor of America has been heard by The Lord, this has become a major part of it's downfall as it has strangled the freedoms of the masses and itself to an unmanageable, gasping dying point. The Senatorial and Congressional pride is in rule and law making, burdensome overregulation of just about every aspect of a miserable, falsely believed life of freedom in the USA. The law and order crowd shout rules and regulations always, which are like a noose around the neck of the American people. Never God's law, the Ten Commandments, but man's strangulating law and order of the masses, the poor and oppressed. The last straw of this strangulation has now been achieved by attempting to strangle the living Church of Jesus Christ, but just as Saul encountered Jesus on the Damascus Road, so will Jesus encounter the USA in His rising fury of a Damascus Road Judgement, they will be blinded and many judgment strikes will be upon them. USA's government is now trying to become the one worshipped, in place of God, as in the days of Nebuchadnezzar's Babylon, but we worship God not government. The U.S. chariot wheels will begin to fall off, it is certain and sure, and has now begun to happen in earnest just as the Bible said, the USA will fall suddenly, like off a precipice.

The ultimate low, the oppression of the poor, the USA polices for profits, asset seizures. (Source); harvardlawreview.org
POLICING AND PROFIT

When residents of Ferguson, Missouri, took to the streets last Au- gust to protest the death of Michael Brown, an unarmed black teenag- er killed by a white police officer, the events dramatically exposed an image of modern policing that most Americans rarely see: columns of police pointing military weaponry at peaceful protestors.1 But the on- going tension between residents and police in Ferguson was also indic- ative of another, less visual development in how the police are used to oppress impoverished communities: using law enforcement to extract revenue from the poor.

In the late 1980s, Missouri became one of the first states to let pri- vate companies purchase the probation systems of local governments.2 In these arrangements, municipalities impose debt on individuals through criminal proceedings and then sell this debt to private busi- nesses, which pad the debt with fees and interest. This debt can stem from fines for offenses as minor as rolling through a stop sign or failing to enroll in the right trash collection service.3 In Ferguson, residents who fall behind on fines and don't appear in court after a warrant is

issued for their arrest (or arrive in court after the court-room doors close, which often happens just five minutes after the session is set to start for the day) are charged an additional $120 to $130 fine, along with a $50 fee for a new arrest warrant and 56 cents for each mile that police drive to serve it.4 Once arrested, everyone who can't pay their fines or post bail (which is usually set to equal the amount of their to- tal debt) is imprisoned until the next court session (which happens three days a month).5 Anyone who is imprisoned is charged $30 to $60 a night by the jail.6 If an arrestee owes fines in more than one of St. Louis County's eighty-one municipal courts, they are passed from one jail to another to await hearings in each town.

The number of these arrests in Ferguson is staggering: in 2013, Ferguson's population was around 21,0007 and its municipal court is- sued 32,975 arrest warrants for nonviolent offenses.8 Ferguson has a per capita income of $20,472, and nearly a quarter of residents and over a third of children live below the poverty line.9 Court fines and fees are Ferguson's second-largest source of income, generating over $2.4 million in revenue in 2013.10 Though many of the towns that sur- round St. Louis draw significant revenue through their courts,11 Ferguson is an outlier: in 2013, its municipal court issued over twice as many arrest warrants per capita as any other town in Missouri.12

Widespread hostility toward Ferguson's municipal court is the tin- der that helped set the town on fire after Michael Brown was killed. Professor Jelani Cobb visited the town just after the shooting and saw this hostility as one of the "intertwined economic and law-enforcement...

***My note,** again, the rich rules over and oppresses the poor, borrowers are slaves to the lenders. The assembly of the wicked runs the show for the controllers.

A Shattered Economy

Dr. Fauci with his team of intellectual fools, with their computer models and science god, along with chief instigator, billionaire vaccine pusher who makes up the Covid 19 patrol has delivered singlehandedly a whopping 32.9% GDP drop to the great USA and the people still has not yet woken up from their slumber. Great Depression 2.0 is already here and no one seems to be aware of it. Now the talk of more lockdowns USA are increasing like wildfire. This will drive the final nail in the US economy casket, and just about kill it. America must be deconstructed before it can be reconstructed, the old must be destroyed before the new can be implemented, out of chaos, order, a new world order must come. This is the plan people, how does one stop this satanic madness? Fast and pray as never before using the minesweeper BIBLE CODE 7.

Lifetimes of the Major Significant Empires

Assyrian Empire 247 years
Persia 208 years
Greece 231 years
Roman Republic 233 years
Roman Empire 207 years
Arab Empire 246 years

Ottoman Empire 250 years
Spain 250 years
Russia 234 years
Britain 250 years
USA 244 years

The USA at 244 years has thrown Jesus off the bus and is almost at an end. Whenever the Bible, Church and family can be destroyed, a nation will stumble and fall also. So listen carefully, the USA will crumble and fall because The Lord has spoken, and all that can be said is, amen. However the fall can be delayed by the mercy cry of our leaders just like Nineveh.

America's biblically Prophecied destruction.

Bel is Confounded, Bel is the same as baal or satan.
Merodach = is Broken, Merodach is a Babylonian idol or god.

Merodach now becomes like satan's left hand man, the prince or chief demon over the USA. These two chief demon gods that rule over America, are anchored in secret societies, going back to the founding of the USA in 1776. Founding President George Washington was a secret society freemason along with many others of the Senate, Congress and US leadership. (Source: George Washington Masonic National Memorial.) Satanic occult rituals were then performed, George Washington even wore his masonic apron to complete the satanic ritual, with the full intention of the USA to produce or spawn the 'son of perdition' or antichrist, that from America he will rule all the nations of the world. This was inserted into the founding of America knowingly by many of it's most prominent leaders and founders. The USA will definitely produce the 'antichrist or son of perdition'. (Evidence, see the U.S. Dollar bill which carries the symbol or mark of the USA along with the mark of satan-the eye of Horus, Isis or Apollo on top of the pyramid, (For camouflage purposes they call it the eye of providence), that same devil who will indwell the son of perdition, antichrist). With over 800 military bases worldwide, enforcement of this plan has already been laid out. America is drunk on power because of these two demons that rule in it. The USA dominates almost the entire world now with over 800 military bases in over 70 nations worldwide with a military budget of over 750 billion dollars. The secret occult destiny and it's intended purpose, the promotion of worship and subservience to this god (Horus, isis, apollo) is secretly hidden behind it's motto,"In God we trust". This referenced god of America in whom it trusts, is the one at the top of the pyramid on it's dollar bill, on one side of the great seal or emblem of the USA, and is the same false god of the old Egyptian empire. America has displayed it's calling card to the whole world, it's money with the god it worships and trusts in, along with it's symbols of worship on it. Above the USA's symbol, the eagle and flag of the USA, are the 13 occult stars in a cloudburst, this they say represents the thirteen colonies.

The true God of America is assumed by the deceived masses to be the one referenced to in the motto, "In God we trust", The God of all gods, Jesus Christ, but this is not so, it is gross deception, as on that same dollar, the god Horus, isis, apollo is openly displayed above the pyramid of the great seal of the USA. By this hidden in plain sight arrangement on the US currency, the USA telegraphs to the whole world, this is the god we trust in and worship, and the world did not believe or recognize it and what it stood for. There was a dual purpose, or dual nature to the USA, one as a good Christian Nation, the good guys, the defenders of freedom, self-determination, democracy with it's many great Christian citizens. While on the dark side, the agenda of hell, the secret societies, the worship, serving and promotion of the other gods was being followed to the very script in the arts, movies, public, social and business arena, almost all mass media, and well camouflaged in all arenas of Government, social, educational and business life. At the first recently contentious mention of separation of Church and State, Jesus was officially ejected from the public Schools, Universities and social arena of the USA, and since that time a rapid descent into hell, into the sewer has begun in earnest. The good Christian side of America is being burnt and not promoted anymore and replaced by the satanic hidden agenda coming to the forefront. Many anti Jesus religions and their people spearheaded the ejection of Jesus from the public discourse. They bought and controlled the major media empires, the disseminators of information in the USA.

But the God of all gods who knows all secrets and has destined a time and method for America's destruction, has revealed here in these CODED Scriptures His intent and judgement. How can America ever escape this judgement? God's people however, will be led out just like Lot was led out from Sodom and Gomorra before it's devastation.

***THE HAMMER OF THE WHOLE EARTH?
How much money has the USA blown on senseless wars?
$1,813 billion dollars since and including the Korean War till now.
How much money has China blown on useless wars? ...$0.00 (Source; Daily Caller. Oct. 16, 2015. Cost of war for each major conflict in US's 239 year history).

The USA is one of the only country in the world that can keep the money printing presses running, along with China.

Constant deficit spending will be one of the key downfalls of the USA, but remember also the roles played by secret societies of wicca, satanist and other dark origins which has riddled the American society, like termites infesting a wooden house. Now let us check all American pride at the door of the Word of God, the Bible, let us understand that God's Word is bigger and more powerful than any nation and it's people or the whole world combined.

The Bible declares that the Medes are God's **chosen avengers**, chosen by God to destroy the USA. The Medes are the people of the Fars region of northwest Iran, the Persians, along with the Iraqis and some portions of Syria and Armenia. The Median Empire of old, encompassed Iran, Iraq, Armenia and parts of Syria and Turkey at the height of their reign. The great general Darius was a Mede. Babylon of old was conquered by the Medes combined with the Persians under Darius's generalship.

Is this why America had chosen to attack Iraq under false pretenses that Saddam Hussein possessed Weapons of Mass Destruction, when Iraq had absolutely none? The USA is continually occupying, and fortifying their positions in Iraq, destabilizing the whole region and are breathing down the Iranians and Syrians back to attack them from this strategic point. The USA has destabilized and weakened this portion of the Middle East, but to no avail, God's Word still stands. No one took time out to read or study the Bible and seek deep understanding from it.

Is it because they don't want God's Word to come to be fulfilled why they have inserted and entrenched themselves in the middle of the Medes territory? If this is their strategy, they are still doomed to failure anyway, as heaven and earth will pass away, but God's Holy Words will never be unfulfilled. The USA is already divided and given to the Medes and other nations of the north regions, and they will surely destroy the USA and there is nothing the USA can do to stop it, except repentance. That demonic territorial Prince of Persia is under God's control only, and no man or nation can bind or control it but Jesus.

A Prophecy concerning Babylon USA's destruction by Prophet Isaiah.

In less than one hundred years the USA went from a Godly Jesus loving nation

Isaiah 47

GOD'S WORD® Translation

1Go, sit in the dirt, virgin princess of Babylon! Sit on the ground, not on a throne, princess of the Babylonians! You will no longer be called soft and delicate.

***The USA is referred to as the Daughter of Babylon, offspring of the first Babylon under king Nebuchadnezzar, proud and delicate.

2Take millstones and grind flour. Remove your veil. Take off your skirt. Uncover your legs, and cross the river.
3People will see you naked. People will see your shame. I will take revenge. I won't spare anyone.

***Babylon will be truly humbled and brought to total shame. God's vengeance is sure.

4Our defender is the Holy One of Israel. His name is the LORD of Armies.

5Go into the dark, and sit in silence, princess of the Babylonians! You will no longer be called the queen of kingdoms.

***A reference that can only be made about the USA, queen of kingdoms. There is no other nation that can claim this title, none. None has received the multitudes of blessings to the extent of the USA.

6I was angry with my people. I dishonored those who belong to me. I put them under your control. You showed them no mercy. You placed a heavy burden on old people.
7You said, "I will always be a queen." You didn't carefully consider these things or keep in mind how they would end.
8Now then, listen to this, you lover of pleasure. You live securely and say to yourself, "I'm the only one, and there's no one else. I won't live as a widow. I won't suffer the loss of children."

***Selfish, arrogant and lover of pleasures. The mistreatment of the believers in Jesus. This mistreatment of God's people is becoming more blatant day by day.

9In one day both of these will happen to you instantly: the loss of your children and your husband. All this will happen to you in spite of your evil magic and your many spells.

***Revealed by The Lord, it's out in the open, the USA is a practitioner of sorcery, it's many wicked magic spells, so says

The Lord, with their gods bel and marduk. In one day, suddenly judgement will come to USA.

10You feel safe in your wickedness and say, "No one can see me." Your wisdom and knowledge have led you astray, so you say to yourself, "I'm the only one, and there's no one else."

***Safety in wickedness with a boastful arrogant attitude. Wisdom knowledge and secret wickedness exposed.

11But evil will happen to you. You won't know how to keep it away. Disaster will strike you. You won't be able to stop it. Destruction will overtake you suddenly. You won't expect it.

***Unstoppable payback, KARMA is coming to USA homeland from God Almighty, suddenly. Evil sown will be evil reaped.

12Keep practicing your spells and your evil magic. You have practiced them ever since you were young. You may succeed. You may cause terror.

***The USA, is a worker and user of evil magic, black and white, sorcery, all evil in God's eyes. **Since you were young**, means that as a newly formed nation in 1776, the USA has been steeped in evil, but because of the God fearing believers God has blessed the USA, in spite of. But evil lurks in it's very foundation.

13You are worn out by your many plans. Let your astrologers and your stargazers, who foretell the future month by month, come to you, rise up, and save you.

***Astrology, Horoscopes, a very large multimillion dollar area of business, centered in the USA with added millions of adherents across the whole world and social strata, especially among the very wealthy, ruling class elites and Hollywood types, the very top social strata of the USA. The ten percenters lead in this arena of Babylon worship, worship of the heavenly hosts. These are the lead adherents with some of the poorer masses following along.

14They are like straw. Fire burns them. They can't rescue themselves from the flames. There are no glowing coals to keep them warm and no fire for them to sit by.
15This is how it will be for those who have worked with you, for those who have been with you ever since you were young. They will go their own ways, and there will be no one to save you.

Thus the Prophet Isaiah was told by God and also saw the destruction of Babylon and recorded it in his book.

The sure destruction of the USA empire, prophecied by Jeremiah the Prophet is also recorded here twice. No coded language here, but straight judgement spoken by God to Jeremiah to reveal to all, the mind of The Lord.

Good News Translation
Jeremiah 50
Babylon's Capture

1 This is the message that the LORD gave me about the
city of Babylon and its people:
2"Tell the news to the nations! Proclaim it!
Give the signal and announce the news!
Do not keep it a secret!
Babylon has fallen!
Her god Marduk has been shattered!
Babylon's idols are put to shame;
her disgusting images are crushed!

*** Babylon USA is a nation of wolves dressed to look like sheep, corrupted from it's founding by many of the founding Fathers who deceived the masses by changing the true God to the demon god Isis–Horus. God's anger is made abundantly clear from the beginning verses here.

3"A nation from the north has come to attack Babylonia
and will make it a desert. People and animals will run
away, and no one will live there."

***A nation from the north, sent by God, from the regions of the north, on a mission to destroy and waste it, the end results, just as God said no one will live there anymore in Babylon USA. A nagging feeling of impending doom is beginning to hang over the USA even now as we witness the great civil unrest occurring in it's cities.

Israel's Return
4The LORD says, "When that time comes, the people
of both Israel and Judah will come weeping, looking for
me, their God. 5They will ask the way to Zion and then
go in that direction. They will make an eternal covenant
with me and never break it.

***Written in Jeremiah's time, he references the people that will come weeping to Jesus Christ as no one can come to God without Him. Millions of Christians will be saved from all nationalities and ethnicities and become one in Jesus Christ. Jeremiah saw the first Babylon and it's destruction, but also Babylon's future daughter, the new Babylon of now, the USA which follows the same path of the old Babylon.

6"My people are like sheep whose shepherds have let them get lost in the mountains. They have wandered like sheep from one mountain to another, and they have forgotten where their home is. 7They are attacked by all who find them. Their enemies say, 'They sinned against the LORD, and so what we have done is not wrong. Their ancestors trusted in the LORD, and they themselves should have remained faithful to him.'

***An indictment from The Lord upon His shepherds who did not teach His sheep properly and allowed them to wander off. An account must be given for these sheep. Jesus Christ will be embraced by all destined for salvation.

8 "People of Israel, run away from Babylonia! Leave the country! Be the first to leave!

***All believers in Jesus, the true Israelites are admonished to leave the USA, Babylon, quickly, go, don't look back. All future financial blessings are to be invested outside of the USA as here in the USA, it will be lost.

9I am going to stir up a group of strong nations in the north and make them attack Babylonia. They will line up in battle against the country and conquer it.

They are skillful hunters, shooting arrows that never miss the mark.

***Babylon USA will bleed from a thousand cuts. It has begun already, God is holding back the fullness of bleeding by His mercies and cries from His chosen children in Jesus. Cuts that will come from a group of strong nations, even nations that are friendly and smile with the USA will stab them in the back, even as Brutus was a stabber and betrayer of Julius Caesar. The USA has many seething, angry secret enemies plotting for its downfall. The leading secret society that controls the whole world's affairs has already given the orders under God's directives. With wide open borders, Babylon USA will surely fall.

10Babylonia will be looted, and those who loot it will take everything they want. I the LORD, have spoken."

Babylon's fall.

***Babylon the plunderer will be plundered, as she has sown, so shall she also reap, national sowing will bring national reaping for Babylon USA the looter and plunderer must fall.

11The LORD says, "People of Babylonia, you plundered my nation. You are happy and glad, going about like a cow threshing grain or like a neighing horse, 12but your own great city will be humiliated and disgraced. Babylonia will be the least important nation of all; it will become a dry and waterless desert.

***Great Babylon that destabilizer of many nations, will now be destabilized, ruined and wasted, reaping from what they have sown is sure.

13Because of my anger no one will live in Babylon; it will be left in ruins, and all who pass by will be shocked and amazed.

14"Archers, line up for battle against Babylon and surround it. Shoot all your arrows at Babylon, because it has sinned against me, the LORD.

***God's personal vendetta against Babylon, they have sinned against Him, vengeance is his and He will surely repay. None shall escape Him. The anger of God burns hot against Babylon because of it's great wickednesses.

15Raise the war cry all around the city! Now Babylon has surrendered. Its walls have been broken through and torn down.+ I am taking my revenge on the Babylonians. So take your revenge on them, and treat them as they have treated others.

***Babylon will see a full view of it's future here, even as it also sees a reflection of it's past of trading it's integrity for access and and success. Only money mattered in all it's arenas of relationships to Babylon, now money is of no help.

16Do not let seeds be planted in that country nor let a harvest be gathered. Every foreigner living there will be afraid of the attacking army and will go back home."

***No seeds planted, no harvest reaped, equals starvation ruin, it is surely coming. The migrant workers will not come to plant or reap the fields.

Revealed here is the fact that there will be skirmishes outbreaks of civil regional wars, fightings in the USA.

Israel's Return

17The LORD says, "The people of Israel are like
sheep, chased and scattered by lions. First, they were
attacked by the emperor of Assyria, and then King
Nebuchadnezzar of Babylonia gnawed on their bones.
18Because of this, I, the LORD Almighty, the God
of Israel, will punish King Nebuchadnezzar and his
country, just as I punished the emperor of Assyria. 19I
will restore the people of Israel to their land. They will
eat the food that grows on Mount Carmel and in the
region of Bashan, and they will eat all they want of the
crops that grow in the territories of Ephraim and Gilead.

***Jeremiah saw an intertwined **dual prophecy**, of old
Babylon under Nebuchadnezzar and another for the coming
future of now Babylon USA. Israel did return to their land from
Babylon past, but now today spiritual Israel will be returning to
Jesus Christ and departing the land of Babylon USA.

20When that time comes, no sin will be found in Israel
and no wickedness in Judah, because I will forgive
those people whose lives I have spared. I, the LORD,
have spoken."

***The righteous that are destined for salvation will be
coming into a reckoning with Jesus the forgiver of all sins of
all persons and we will all become ONE in Him.

God's Judgment on Babylonia

21The LORD says, "Attack the people of Merathaim
and of Pekod. Kill and destroy them.+ Do everything
I command you. I, the LORD, have spoken. 22The
noise of battle is heard in the land, and there is great

destruction. 23Babylonia hammered the whole world to pieces, and now that hammer is shattered! All the nations are shocked at what has happened to that country.

***Babylon USA which had full spectrum dominance over all nations of the earth has now been checkmated by The Lord Himself using His chosen nations to destroy the USA with it's 800 plus military bases all over the world and it's massive military might. The USA fought against God by rebelling against Him in every conceivable way, ending in the pit of sodomy, child sacrifices, astrology and many other immoralities. We tracked how the first Babylon, Shinar was in rebellious perverted worship, with child sacrifices and all types of immoralities. All the previous four Babylon's were utterly wasted and so will Babylon number five, the USA.

24Babylonia, you fought against me, and you have been caught in the trap I set for you, even though you did not know it. 25 I have opened the place where my weapons are stored, and in my anger I have taken them out, because I, the Sovereign LORD Almighty, have work to do in Babylonia.

***Fighting against God is a no win situation, God's traps will always catch His hapless victims. But God has weaponry, an arsenal, a bunker to keep His weapons, then in anger and to do His absolute will He will execute His fury upon Babylon USA.

26Attack it from every side and break open the places where its grain is stored! Pile up the loot like piles of grain! Destroy the country! Leave nothing at all! 27Kill all their soldiers! Slaughter them! The people of

Babylonia are doomed! The time has come for them to be punished!"

***Extremely dire and angry words from the Living God against USA Babylon, there is no escape, utter destruction is coming for their sins against God. Just like Jericho (Babylon), Babylon USA will meet the same fate. Kill and destroy them, the marching orders from God. Babylon has become an abomination to God, just like Sodom and Gomorrah, Jericho and Belshazzar's Babylon.

(28Refugees escape from Babylonia and come to Jerusalem, and they tell how the LORD our God took revenge for what the Babylonians had done to his Temple.)
29 "Tell the archers to attack Babylon. Send out everyone who knows how to use the bow and arrow. Surround the city and don't let anyone escape. Pay it back for all it has done, and treat it as it has treated others, because it acted with pride against me, the Holy One of Israel.

***Proud Babylon with it's pride marches scoffing at God, now an awful swift payback. Retribution to the max. Just as the USA sanctioned and embargoed, surrounded, other nations who it disagrees with, so will God sanction and embargo the USA, none will escape, return to it what it has done to others. KARMA- payback time has come for it. The Word of God declares that if our very enemies are hungry, we should feed them, and if thirsty, give them to drink. USA has embargoed even the very medically necessary equipment and medicines to several nations it disagrees with, USA is playing God.

30So its young men will be killed in the city streets, and all its soldiers will be destroyed on that day. I, the LORD, have spoken.

31"Babylonia, you are filled with pride, so I, the Sovereign LORD Almighty, am against you! The time has come for me to punish you. 32Your proud nation will stumble and fall, and no one will help you up. I will set your cities on fire, and everything around will be destroyed."

***God detests pride, haughtiness. All the sodomite proud and haughty will be destroyed before The Lord.

Rationality is departing and an irrationality is seizing the minds of many so called intelligent people in the forefront of our society today. Our leaders national and international, have become very irrational. Their minds are failing them because of that demon of fear. God's people however will not be on a power trip, even though God gave us a spirit of power, but on an authority trip, a trip knowing our names are written in the book of life and that we are seated with Jesus in heavenly places. We thereby proclaim His Lordship not only in our lives, but in the rulership of this entire world, we will occupy till He comes. We can already see that the US cities are on fire of hell with looting, murders, robberies and many are making a hasty exit from these cities.

33The LORD Almighty says, "The people of Israel and of Judah are oppressed. All who captured them are guarding them closely and will not let them go. 34But the one who will rescue them is strong—his name is the LORD Almighty. He himself will take up their cause

and will bring peace to the earth, but trouble to the people of Babylonia."
35The LORD says,
"Death to Babylonia!
Death to its people,
to its rulers, to its people of wisdom.
36Death to its lying prophets—
what fools they are!
Death to its soldiers—
how terrified they are!

***A horrible condemnation of death to an unrepentant people. The only way out, or reversal is repentance and a mercy cry before the living God

God prophecies death to all in Babylon USA also to the lying prophets, those who should know better, but have sold out Jesus for 30 pieces of silver, or less, prophesying and promoting everything and everyone else but Jesus Christ.

37Destroy its horses and chariots!
Death to its hired soldiers—
how weak they are!
Destroy its treasures;
plunder and loot.

***The Assets, Contractors, mercenaries hired guns of the USA will surely die.

Plunder the USA because it is a plunderer. The USA has plundered the Iraqi gold and oil, the Syrian oilfields, Afghanistan resources, Care Act monies from the needy poor Main Street families plundered by the wealthy. In every arena USA is a plunderer and will now be plundered.

38Bring a drought on its land
and dry up its rivers.
Babylonia is a land of terrifying idols
that have made fools of the people.
39 "And so Babylon will be haunted by demons and
evil spirits,+ and by unclean birds. Never again will
people live there, not for all time to come. 40 The same
thing will happen to Babylon that happened to Sodom
and Gomorrah, when I destroyed them and the nearby
towns. No one will ever live there again. I, the LORD,
have spoken.

*****Same as Sodom and Gomorrah? God will do a Sodom
and Gomorrah judgement job on the USA. Why? Sodomy,
homosexuality, Babylon worship, child -human sacrifices,
bestiality is an abomination to Him.**

41"People are coming from a country in the north,
a mighty nation far away;
many kings are preparing for war.
42They have taken their bows and swords;
they are cruel and merciless.
They sound like the roaring sea,
as they ride their horses.
They are ready for battle against Babylonia.

***The swarming strategy of using a horrendous mass of
humans to swarm all across the land. Cruel, merciless people
coming to destroy Babylon.

43The king of Babylonia hears the news,
and his hands hang limp.
He is seized by anguish,

by pain like a woman in labor.

44"Like a lion coming out of the thick woods along the Jordan up to the green pasture land, I, the LORD, will come and make the Babylonians run away suddenly from their city. Then the leader I choose will rule the nation. Who can be compared to me? Who would dare challenge me? What ruler could oppose me? 45So listen to the plan that I have made against the city of Babylon and to what I intend to do to its people. Even their children will be dragged off, and everyone will be horrified. 46When Babylon falls, there will be such a noise that the entire earth will shake, and the cries of alarm will be heard by the other nations."

***The President will hear of this horrible news and is dumfounded, perplexed, with no solutions, all his hope is gone he has given up.

The powerful plan of God to suddenly, totally destroy Babylon USA because of it's pride, sodomy and babies murdered.

This is Jeremiah's first chapter of God's judgement upon Babylon, chapter two follows right behind.

The world is run by people we know, elected officials, but controlled by people we'll never see or know.

Jeremiah 52
Good News Translation
Further Judgment on Babylonia

1The LORD says, "I am bringing a destructive wind+ against Babylonia and its people. 2I will send foreigners to destroy Babylonia like a wind that blows straw away.

When that day of destruction comes, they will attack from every side and leave the land bare.

***Embedded sleeper cells waiting for a signal to rise up and attack the USA from within, they are already here waiting for the right time and signal. Hamas, ISIS, MS 13? The leader will be the Medes and their allies.

3Don't give its soldiers time to shoot their arrows or to put on their armor. Do not spare the young men! Destroy the whole army! 4They will be wounded and die in the streets of their cities. 5I, the LORD God Almighty, have not abandoned Israel and Judah, even though they have sinned against me, the Holy One of Israel.

***the element of surprise, the suddenness of rising up upon a given signal to destroy just as God said, suddenly. God will never forget His children the faithful to Jesus, the chosen ones.

6Run away from Babylonia! Run for your lives! Do not be killed because of Babylonia's sin. I am now taking my revenge and punishing it as it deserves.

***ATTENTION WARNING, all Christians leave Babylon USA now or else die,(You'll go to heaven, but die) run for your lives. God's revenge and punishment is coming. When? I don't know, but it's coming for sure.
Note: Babylon USA can be departed from, but new world order one world Babylon is also here.

7 Babylonia was like a gold cup in my hand, making the whole world drunk. The nations drank its wine and went out of their minds. 8Babylonia has suddenly fallen

and is destroyed! Mourn over it! Get medicine for its wounds, and maybe it can be healed. 9 Foreigners living there said, 'We tried to help Babylonia, but it was too late. Let's leave now and go back home. God has punished Babylonia with all his might and has destroyed it completely.'"

***God has spoken and said the USA cannot be saved, it's not salvageable, so leave now, jump the leaking ship because it's doomed. It has reached a point of no return and must be destroyed as all four Babylon's before it. No mercy will be shown to it and it will go down to be utterly wasted and destroyed just as Sodom and Gomorrah was. Sodom and Gomorrah behavior equals Sodom and Gomorrah destruction. The engineering of the destruction has been done by a centralized organization to destroy the USA. This organization has to be greater than the USA itself, and must be a global organization that controls the world's nations. This is a secret organization that controls the whole world and is controlled by just a few unseen and unknown trillionaire which are in charge. The real boss, however, is Jesus Christ who is in ultimate control and He has determined it's doom with all His might.

The misery index inside the USA and the world will rise quickly and broadly across all spectrums of the masses social affairs. This will cause a rapid rise in poverty, homelessness eventually riots and a large outmigration of people from the USA. People of another nationality living in the USA will reason, why stay here and suffer, why sit here till we die? I have a better or greater chance of survival in my native country, I won't starve there. Or I would rather suffer and die in my own country, so I will leave the USA and go home to my native land. God has said, "Come out from among them", and they will.

10The LORD says, "My people shout, 'The LORD has shown that we are in the right. Let's go and tell the people in Jerusalem what the LORD our God has done.'" 11The LORD has stirred up the kings of Media, because he intends to destroy Babylonia. That is how he will take revenge for the destruction of his Temple.

The attacking officers command, "Sharpen your arrows! Get your shields ready!

***The kings of Media stirred up? Just like Belshazzar's Babylon four, was attacked by the Medes and Persians, the Iranians, will this coming attack involve Iran also? The Persians? They are the only nation that stands up to the USA's many threats without fear, intimidation, never backing down. Again, is this why the USA has wedged itself in Iraq to ward off or blunt this threat? To bind or control the prince of Persia?

12Give the signal to attack Babylon's walls. Strengthen the guard! Post the sentries! Place troops in ambush!" The LORD has done what he said he would do to the people of Babylonia. 13 That country has many rivers and rich treasures, but its time is up, and its thread of life is cut.

***Certainly not a reference to Iraq, old Babylon, but the daughter of Babylon the USA, with it's many rivers, and rich treasures. A perfect code, a giveaway as to the identity of who this Babylon really is, the USA definitely is the modern day Babylon.

Now it's thread of life is cut, it's over, nothing can stop it's death, except maybe a mercy cry from it's leaders just like Nineveh's leader did.

14The LORD Almighty has sworn by his own life that he will bring many men to attack Babylonia like a swarm of locusts, and they will shout with victory.

***God swearing by His own life? This is deadly, a very serious oath by God. Swarming like locusts, the Chinese has 1.4 billion people, surely they will be one of the nations involved in the USA's takedown. This spells out the strategy that will be used to takedown Babylon USA, the swarming technique, the victory shout will be given by them as they defeat the USA.

A Hymn of Praise to God
15The LORD made the earth by his power;
by his wisdom he created the world
and stretched out the heavens.
16At his command the waters above the sky+ roar;
he brings clouds from the ends of the earth.
He makes lightning flash in the rain
and sends the wind from his storeroom.
17At the sight of this, people feel stupid and senseless;
those who make idols are disillusioned
because the gods they make are false and lifeless.
18They are worthless and should be despised;
they will be destroyed when the LORD comes to deal
with them.
19The God of Jacob is not like them;
he is the one who made everything,
and he has chosen Israel to be his very own people.
The LORD Almighty is his name.

***A testament of Gods might and power, His absolute authority and choosing of the Jewish people until Jesus came.

Upon Jesus's coming one needed no more to be a Jew with a genealogical trace, but to be only in Jesus, through the spiritual DNA to be called Israel, to be part of spiritual Israel, one must only be born again.

The LORD's Hammer
20The LORD says,
"Babylonia, you are my hammer, my weapon of war.
I used you to crush nations and kingdoms,
21to shatter horses and riders,
to shatter chariots and their drivers,
22to kill men and women,
to slay old and young,
to kill boys and girls,
23to slaughter shepherds and their flocks,
to slaughter farmers and their plow horses,
to crush rulers and high officials."

***Surely The Lord used USA as a **HAMMER and weapon of war**, across the nations of the world, but the USA became arrogant, proud and a serial war aggressor, not listening to it's master Jesus, but in rebellion against Him. Another coded reference to Babylon USA.

Babylonia's Punishment
24The LORD says, "You will see me repay Babylonia and its people for all the evil they did to Jerusalem. 25Babylonia, you are like a mountain that destroys the whole world, but I, the LORD, am your enemy. I will take hold of you, level you to the ground, and leave you in ashes. 26None of the stones from your ruins will ever

be used again for building. You will be like a desert forever. I, the LORD, have spoken.

***Only the USA has controlled or destroyed by it's influence the whole world in one way or another, by war or by Wall Street, International Monetary Funds finance or by encouraging and enforcing sodomy and abortion on the nations thereof. Another coded reference to Babylon USA, the evil they did to the Christians and their Churches, referred to as Jerusalem, city of peace, Babylon and it's people surely will repay.

27"Give the signal to attack! Blow the trumpet so that the nations can hear! Prepare the nations for war against Babylonia! Tell the kingdoms of Ararat, Minni, and Ashkenaz to attack. Appoint an officer to lead the attack. Bring up the horses like a swarm of locusts. 28Prepare the nations for war against Babylonia. Send for the kings of Media, their leaders and officials, and the armies of all the countries they control.

***The kings of the Medes are surely coming along with their other workmates the Persians. This sounds like Belshazzar's Babylon destruction all over again. This is God's final checkmate for Babylon USA.

29The earth trembles and shakes because the LORD is carrying out his plan to make Babylonia a desert, where no one lives. 30The Babylonian soldiers have stopped fighting and remain in their forts. They have lost their courage and have become helpless. The city gates are broken down, and the houses are on fire. 31Messenger after messenger runs to tell the king of Babylonia that his city has been broken into from every side. 32The

enemy have captured the river crossing and have set
the fortresses on fire. The Babylonian soldiers have
panicked. 33Soon the enemy will cut them down and
trample them like grain on a threshing place. I, the
LORD Almighty, the God of Israel, have spoken."

***The terror of God will strike Babylon USA.

34The king of Babylonia cut Jerusalem up
and ate it.
He emptied the city like a jar;
like a monster he swallowed it.
He took what he wanted
and threw the rest away.
35Let the people of Zion say,
"May Babylonia be held responsible
for the violence done to us!"
Let the people of Jerusalem say,
"May Babylonia be held responsible
for what we have suffered!"
The LORD Will Help Israel
36And so the LORD said to the people of Jerusalem,
"I will take up your cause and will make your enemies
pay for what they did to you. I will dry up the source of
Babylonia's water and make its rivers go dry.

***Babylon five was entered into just as God said here, the
waters were dried up and the army of Darius walked in the dry
river bed and entered Babylon at night and took the city by surprise. The Lord will help Israel, His chosen ones, the believers
in Jesus Christ.

37That country will become a pile of ruins where wild animals live. It will be a horrible sight; no one will live there, and all who see it will be terrified. 38The Babylonians all roar like lions and growl like lion cubs. 39Are they greedy? I will prepare them a feast and make them drunk and happy. They will go to sleep and never wake up.

***The Babylonians roar like lions and growl like lion cubs, all fake, just like satanic infused people, going around like a roaring lion seeking whom he may devour. The real lions are the Christians with the Lion of the tribe of Judah, Jesus, indwelling them.

God's master strategy, make them like drunken men, greedy, sleeping and never rising. This is the God factor from which there is no hiding place.

Drunkenness has overtaken the USA, spiritual and mental through substances, delusional drunkenness to believe they can mock God and evade Him and physical drunkenness of drugs, alcohol and by lethargy and physical incapacitations.

40I will take them to be slaughtered, like lambs, goats, and rams. I, the LORD, have spoken."

***Just like Babylon 5 in the days of king Belshazzar, there was a riotous feast and party, an orgy of anything and everything goes. In the midst of the party when they were well drunk, they chose to bring out the golden vessels that were used to minister before the Lord in the Temple in Jerusalem. Note now God says He will make them drunk and happy, from which they will never wake up. God will make sure they are set up for a sure fall and kill, He has commanded death to Babylon USA, just as he did before.

Babylon's Fate

41The LORD says about Babylon: "The city that the whole world praised has been captured! What a horrifying sight Babylon has become to the nations! 42The sea has rolled over Babylon and covered it with roaring waves. 43The towns have become a horrifying sight and are like a waterless desert, where no one lives or even travels. 44I will punish Bel, the god of Babylonia, and make him give up his stolen goods; the nations will not worship him any more.

"Babylon's walls have fallen.

***The whole world praises this city, tourists from around the world comes here. New York city. Message to all God's people, run away from Babylon USA very quickly.

45People of Israel, run away from there! Run for your life from my fierce anger. 46Do not lose courage or be afraid because of the rumors you hear. Every year a different rumor spreads—rumors of violence in the land and of one king fighting another.

***This is the time we are in now. Civil uprising and discord in USA all across the nation, the architect is Jesus The Lord himself, just as His Word says. This is a whip or scourge to uproot the Christians and for them to see about getting out of the USA. RUN FOR YOUR LIVES! Violence and civil fighting.

47And so the time is coming when I will deal with Babylonia's idols. The whole country will be put to shame, and all its people will be killed. 48 Everything on earth and in the sky will shout for joy when Babylonia falls to the people who come from the north to destroy it. 49 Babylonia caused the death of people all over the world, and now Babylonia will fall because it caused the death of so many Israelites. I, the LORD, have spoken."

***USA's crime, here stated by God. The wars of US aggression worldwide will be paid back in one swoop. All the dead across the world will be avenged.

God's Message to the Israelites in Babylonia

50The LORD says to his people in Babylonia: "You have escaped death! Now go! Don't wait! Though you are far from home, think about me, your LORD, and remember Jerusalem. 51You say, 'We've been disgraced and made ashamed; we feel completely helpless because foreigners have taken over the holy places in the Temple.' 52So then, I say that the time is coming when I will deal with Babylon's idols, and the wounded will groan throughout the country.

***God's message to His people who believe on Jesus Christ in Babylon USA, you will escape death, but leave now. It is I who calls you out of Babylon, now go, don't wait my people.

No matter what type of security apparatus Babylon employs, it is doomed.

53Even if Babylon could climb to the sky and build a strong fortress there, I would still send people to destroy it. I, the LORD, have spoken."

Further Destruction on Babylon

54The LORD says,

"Listen to the sound of crying in Babylon,

of mourning for the destruction in the land.

***The weeping, mourning lamenting of the American people, but alas, it's too late now. They refused to believe that mighty USA with all it's military power could be brought down. They refused to submit to Jesus Christ and so God punished them for their pride and arrogance. Pride still goes before a fall and a haughty spirit before destruction.

55I am destroying Babylon
and putting it to silence.
The armies rush in like roaring waves
and attack with noisy shouts.

***The swarming technique will be employed led by The Lord Himself against the USA. Like roaring waves, masses of human enemies swarming over the land. China's population of 1.4 billion people is their weapon of mass destruction. An old Chinese story was told and goes like this. One day China and the USA will meet on a very narrow road fit for only one person, and only one person will survive. In the eyes of the Chinese that survivor will be China. In the eyes of God it will not be the USA.

56They have come to destroy Babylon;
its soldiers are captured,
and their bows are broken.
I am a God who punishes evil,
and I will treat Babylon as it deserves.
57I will make its rulers drunk—
men of wisdom, leaders, and soldiers.
They will go to sleep and never wake up.
I, the king, have spoken;

I am the LORD Almighty.

***Stupor drunk leaders, drunk on pride, on stupidity, at all levels making foolish decisions. KARMA, payback reaping prevails.

58The walls of mighty Babylon will be thrown to
the ground,
and its towering gates burned down.
The work of the nations is all for nothing;
their efforts go up in flames.
I, the LORD Almighty, have spoken."

***Final will and Word of God, like it or not this is His will and word.

Jeremiah's Message Is Sent to Babylonia
59King Zedekiah's personal attendant was Seraiah, the son of Neriah and grandson of Mahseiah. In the fourth year that Zedekiah was king of Judah, Seraiah was going to Babylonia with him, and I gave him some instructions. 60I wrote in a book an account of all the destruction that would come on Babylonia, as well as all these other things about Babylonia. 61I told Seraiah, "When you get to Babylon, be sure to read aloud to the people everything that is written here. 62Then pray, 'LORD, you have said that you would destroy this place, so that there would be no living creatures in it, neither people nor animals, and it would be like a desert forever.' 63 Seraiah, when you finish reading this book to the people, then tie it to a rock and throw it into the Euphrates River 64and say, 'This is what will happen to

Babylonia—it will sink and never rise again because of the destruction that the LORD is going to bring on it.'"+ The words of Jeremiah end here.

The subverted USA.
Subverted by outsiders, anti Christians.

In 1608, a congregation of disgruntled English Protestants from the village of Scrooby, Nottinghamshire, left England and moved to Leyden, a town in Holland. These "Separatists" did not want to pledge allegiance to the Church of England, which they believed was nearly as corrupt and idolatrous as the Catholic Church it had replaced, any longer. (They were not the same as the Puritans, who had many of the same objections to the English church but wanted to reform it from within.) The Separatists hoped that in Holland, they would be free to worship as they liked.

In fact, the Separatists, or "Saints," as they called themselves, did find religious freedom in Holland, but they also found a very immoral secular life that was more difficult for them and their children to navigate than they'd anticipated. So by God's mighty hand they were able to journey to the New World the USA. After many difficult hardships, bitter cold winters, sicknesses, deaths of many of their numbers, and numerous prayers, they were finally able to plant, reap food and turn the corner of adversity from sickness to health, from insufficiencies to plenty with God's mighty hand of help. God gave them favor with the Indian populations they met in Massachusetts, who in turn helped them to survive there and without whose help they might not have made it.

By November 21, 1620, after the Colonies grew and became stronger, the Mayflower Compact was signed, the

USA Pilgrim Leaders covenanting the new USA and it's people with God Almighty.

The USA however, is not a Christian nation anymore, it started out that way by the Pilgrims, but by the official Founding in 1776, July 4th, the USA was subverted, hijacked and given over to the Freemason's god Isis or Horus. America started out as a Christian nation, but upon the Declaration of it's Independence in 1776 and the adoption of the great seal of the USA June 20, 1782, it was totally subverted.

By June 20, 1782 one hundred and sixty two years later, the Godly USA was subverted and overthrown by secret satanists of secret societies, who deceived the founding Fathers, who now issued and proclaimed in open secret another god for the USA to follow and serve. Wealthy satanists that came from the European old world to the new world with an agenda of a new world order, ultimate Babylon global vision. The USA was now undermined by secret societies and satanic practices that was now birthed and entrenched in the USA.

Stealth was employed at the top tiers of Government to bring it under satanic control, truly fulfilling satan's plan to sit on the mount (very pinnacle) of the congregation, this newly formed covenanted nation under God. What a difference a hundred and sixty two years makes in history.

The great seal of the USA was now made and adopted in 1782. The god Isis–Horus as seen and depicted by the single eye at the top of the pyramid on the great seal of the USA's one dollar bill, also by the 13 stars above the eagle on the opposite side of the seal. The USA's current god is very visible on the one dollar bill, The Great Seal. This was placed on the dollar bill in 1935 by President Roosevelt.

The number thirteen is a satanically coded number and stands for rebellion;

Genesis 14

4 Twelve years they served Chedorlaomer, and in the thirteenth year they rebelled.

This was a telegraphed calling card that there was a take-over, a switch, an overthrow of the God of the Pilgrims, God of the Bible, the True and only God and another god was chosen for official worship in the USA of the satanist's doing. The flag, emblem name and symbol was now openly shown and declared, yet the eyes of the American nation and it's people were shut and their understanding darkened. In plain sight the god Horus, Isis, apollo (all the same god) satan was now declared and enthroned as god of the newly formed USA, in that god we trust. The downfall of the USA was now begun, however one day with The Lord is like a thousand years, the USA Empire as of now is only 244 years old. 1776-2020. The longest lasting empires were about 250 years, maybe in six years it's over for the U.S.? Only God knows.

The USA was now declared as that nation to birth or bring forth the anti-Christ the son of perdition spoken of in the Book of Revelation, all moves are going forward to accomplish this. Let's examine carefully the top pyramid above the bottom pyramid. The top pyramid depicts those whose eyes have been opened to and allowed to enter that secret society, the exclusive club of satan. This is done through many secret societies, clubs , brotherhoods, sisterhoods with secret initiation rites and rituals. Proverbs 22 vs. 7 Declares that, **"the rich rules over the poor and the borrower is slave to the lender." Never forget this as this is the world's business model for all nations.**

This depiction from the Great seal tells the whole story of the ruling class rich ruling over the masses and the poor foolish ones who doesn't have a clue as to what is going on. But

Jesus is working to bring revelation knowledge to the chosen ones that He will lead out of bondage and destruction. Fast forward to July 2020, the major corporations have now issued a decree, usurping the Federal State and Local Governments, a mandatory mask wearing. This rule by them overturns the Government, elected representatives control and regulations of corporations, now the corporations have overridden the Government and representatives and will further issue decrees to control the masses while the worthless Government stands idly by. All this is sudden, new, mandatory must be obeyed or no buying, so will it be when satan's mark is to be implemented. The USA will be subverted and suddenly, once again.

A Prophecy from John the Revelator regarding Babylon USA's Destruction.

Revelation 17

GOD'S WORD® Translation

1One of the seven angels who held the seven bowls came and said to me, "Come, I will show you the judgment of that notorious prostitute who sits on raging waters. 2The kings of the earth had sex with her, and those living on earth became drunk on the wine of her sexual sins." 3Then the angel carried me by his power into the wilderness. I saw a woman sitting on a bright red beast covered with insulting names. It had seven heads and ten horns. 4The woman wore purple clothes, bright red clothes, gold jewelry, gems, and pearls. In her hand she was holding a gold cup filled with detestable and evil things from her sexual sins. 5A name was written on her forehead. The name was Mystery: Babylon the Great, the Mother of Prostitutes and Detestable Things of the Earth. 6I saw that the woman was drunk with the blood of God's holy people and of those who testify about Jesus. I was very surprised when I saw her.

7The angel asked me, "Why are you surprised? I will tell you the mystery of the woman and the beast with the seven heads and the ten horns that carries her.

8"You saw the beast which once was, is no longer, and will come from the bottomless pit and go to its destruction. Those living on earth, whose names were not written in the Book of Life when the world was created, will be surprised when they see the beast because it was, is no longer, and will come again. **9**"In this situation a wise mind is needed. The seven heads are seven mountains on which the woman is sitting. **10**They are also seven kings. Five of them have fallen, one is ruling now, and the other has not yet come. When he comes, he must remain for a little while. **11**The beast that was and is no longer is the eighth king. It belongs with the seven kings and goes to its destruction. **12**"The ten horns that you saw are ten kings who have not yet started to rule. They will receive authority to rule as kings with the beast for one hour. **13**They have one purpose-to give their power and authority to the beast.

14They will go to war against the lamb. The lamb will conquer them because he is Lord of lords and King of kings. Those who are called, chosen, and faithful are with him."

15The angel also said to me, "The waters you saw, on which the prostitute is sitting, are people, crowds, nations, and languages. **16**The ten horns and the beast you saw will hate the prostitute. They will leave her abandoned and naked. They will eat her flesh and burn her up in a fire. **17**God has made them do what he wants them to do. So they will give their kingdom to the beast until God's words are carried out. **18**The woman you saw is the important city which dominates the kings of the earth."

Revelation 18
GOD'S WORD® Translation

1After these things I saw another angel come from heaven. He had tremendous power, and his glory lit up the earth. **2**He cried out in a powerful voice, "Fallen! Babylon the Great has fallen! She has become a home for demons. She is a prison for every evil spirit, every unclean bird, and every unclean and hated beast. **3**All the nations fell because of the wine of her sexual sins. The kings of the earth had sex with her. Her luxurious wealth has made the merchants of the earth rich."

4I heard another voice from heaven saying, "Come out of Babylon, my people, so that you do not participate in her sins and suffer from any of her plagues. **5**Her sins are piled as high as heaven, and God has remembered her crimes. **6**Do to her what she has done. Give her twice as much as she gave. Serve her a drink in her own cup twice as large as the drink she served others. **7**She gave herself glory and luxury. Now give her just as much torture and misery. She says to herself, 'I'm a queen on a throne, not a widow. I'll never be miserable.' **8**For this reason her plagues of death, misery, and starvation will come in a single day. She will be burned up in a fire, because the Lord God, who judges her, is powerful.

9"The kings of the earth who had sex with her and lived in luxury with her will cry and mourn over her when they see the smoke rise from her raging fire. **10**Frightened by her torture, they will stand far away and say, 'How horrible, how horrible it is for that important city, the powerful city Babylon! In one moment judgment has come to it!'

11"The merchants of the earth cry and mourn over her, because no one buys their cargo anymore. **12**No one buys their cargo of gold, silver, gems, pearls, fine linen, purple cloth, silk, bright red cloth, all kinds of citron wood, articles made of ivory and very costly wood, bronze, iron, marble, **13**cinnamon, spices, incense, perfume, frankincense, wine, olive oil, flour, wheat, cattle, sheep, horses, wagons, slaves (that is, humans). **14**'The fruit you craved is gone. All your luxuries and your splendor have disappeared. No one will ever find them again.' **15**"Frightened by her torture, the merchants who had become rich by selling these things will stand far away. They will cry and mourn, **16**saying, 'How horrible, how horrible for that important city which was wearing fine linen, purple clothes, bright red clothes, gold jewelry, gems, and pearls. **17**In one moment all this wealth has been destroyed!' Every ship's captain, everyone who traveled by ship, sailors, and everyone who made their living from the sea stood far away. **18**When they saw the smoke rise from her raging fire, they repeatedly cried out, 'Was there ever a city as important as this?' **19**Then they threw dust on their heads and shouted while crying and mourning, 'How horrible, how horrible for that important city. Everyone who had a ship at sea grew rich because of that city's high prices. In one moment it has been destroyed!'

20"Gloat over it, heaven, God's people, apostles, and prophets. God has condemned it for you."
21Then a powerful angel picked up a stone that was like a large millstone. He threw it into the sea and said, "The important city Babylon will be thrown down with the same force. It will never be found again. **22**The sound of harpists, musicians, flutists, and trumpeters will never be heard in it again. Skilled craftsman will never be found in it again. The sound of a millstone will never be heard in it again. **23**Light from lamps will never shine in it again. Voices of brides and grooms will never be heard in it again. Its merchants were the important people of the world, because all the nations were deceived by its witchcraft. **24**"The blood of prophets, God's people, and everyone who had been murdered on earth was found in it."

***Until this very day most people of the USA are settled in, complacent and do not have even a clue as to what the hidden in plain sight message is on the very money they spend so often. It has grown worse as today paper money is only 3% of use in the USA, 97% of money used is digital currency.

On the world's front the USA is now on trial because of it's blatant discrimination against African Americans and other minorities. Lets not forget the American Indians, the first Americans.

Four major heinous crimes committed against humanity in and by America were;
    1—The American Indian massacre i.e Wounded Knee. (1990 US Congress did pass a resolution expressing Deep Regrets for this massacre.)

2—Uncompensated slavery since the year 1619 of African Americans.

3—Abortions of over 65 million babies in USA since Roe vs. Wade. (Law enacted by the Supreme Court in 1973. Infant sacrifices to the demon god moloch or marduk)

4—The legalization of homosexuality in June 2016.

The US administrations have always had smart intelligent men and women there in key leadership positions, however this is the major shortcoming of the USA and all nations of the world, too many intelligent people but they lack wise people in key leadership and advisory positions.

Wisdom begins with the fear of God but never ends. So one must continually be a God fearing person which means they must be a Christian, as there is no other way to God without Jesus Christ the way and door.

This is a specific targeted word God gave me regarding the greedy billionaires buying up homes to make renters, serfs out of the masses of people. Woe be unto them...

Isaiah 5 Contemporary English Bible

8You are in for trouble! You take over house after house and field after field, until there is no room left for anyone else in all the land. 9But the LORD All-Powerful has made this promise to me:

Those large and beautiful homes will be left empty, with no one to take care of them. 10Four hectares of grape-vines will produce only 27 liters of juice, and 180 liters of seed will produce merely 18 liters of grain.

11 You are in for trouble! You get up early to start drinking, and you keep it up late into the night. 12At

your drinking parties you have the music of stringed instruments, tambourines, and flutes. But you never even think about all the LORD has done, 13and so his people know nothing about him. That's why many of you will be dragged off to foreign lands. Your leaders will starve to death, and everyone else will suffer from thirst.

21You think you are clever and smart. 22And you are great at drinking and mixing drinks. But you are in for trouble. 23You accept bribes to let the guilty go free, and you cheat the innocent out of a fair trial.

24You will go up in flames like straw and hay! You have rejected the teaching of the holy LORD God All-Powerful of Israel. Now your roots will rot, and your blossoms will turn to dust.

25You are the LORD's people, but you made him terribly angry, and he struck you with his mighty arm. Mountains shook, and dead bodies covered the streets like garbage. The LORD is still angry, and he is ready to strike you again.+

***What they and the USA has sown, it shall surely reap. The contaminated USA, has been overtaken by evil people that has caused it to stumble and it will surely fall. Escaping Babylon USA, however, is not escaping Jesus the Righteous Judge.

Weakness invites, begs aggression

The theory and practice of oligarchic, ruling class rulership is to make things much harder than they need to be for the people, the masses, so that when they cry out, any concession or any let up that is given, the ruling class will look so great, they seem like a hero or deliverer. They look good.

This is the optics they portray, that of a benevolent master looking over the slaves, those not in the top ten percent and members of the clubs.

Prov. 22, Again..

7 "The rich rules over the poor, borrower is slave to the lender"

7Poor people are slaves of the rich. Borrow money and you are the lender's slave.

Strategy of the wealthy, is to keep the masses on the back foot. Unbalanced and off guard. As long as they can do this they will continue to rule, they will dominate, but we the believers who weaponize the Word of God using the sword of the spirit, dominate in the name of Jesus, we occupy until He returns, we bind it here and He binds it there, we loose it here He looses it there. When God's children come into full understanding of this, they will begin to see the authority that they carry. BIBLE CODE 7 is to bring you into that realm of understanding so you can wield your God given power and authority.

Make your plan of escape from Babylon USA, The Lord says.

A revelation from God on 6/25/2020 @ 0055 hrs.
An African American USA Prophecy

A black *EXODUS from THE USA* is coming. You might call it Blaxit.

America will eventually give reparations to the descendants of slavery.

Upon these reparations being paid out, something dynamic will happen in the USA and many will leave in a repatriation move to Africa, to go back to Ghana, Nigeria and other nations there, but primarily Ghana to permanently live, where they will be openly embraced, millions will go, return to many nations in Africa and the Islands. It will be a shock to many, racist uprisings from whites will fuel the fire and this will be a driving force for many blacks to get out of the USA. This will be the equivalent of leaving Egypt by the Hebrews led by Moses. This is the fulfilling of the Word of God which we have already gone through in the Book of Jeremiah. The spirit of Marcus Garvey the Jamaican leader will rise up once again to bring about this event. God will raise up a new leader to spearhead this massive move of population and fight against the backlash of others.

The multi generational curse of colonialism-slavery-apartheid.

The multi century looting and plundering of the black slaves lives, labor, descendants and future, 250 years of slavery and afterwards since emancipation, the constant, perpetual looting and plundering of their wealth, labor, material possessions, peace, joy, security and future.

Reparations will be paid to the black slave descendants, **'just as I paid my children in Egypt and they left Egypt with money so will my children leave USA with money to go back to the Motherland Africa.**

I will make her leaders drunk and sleep, they will surely pay, says the Lord'.

In light of the Floyd murder, a black house cleaning project must be initiated. This cannot be business just as usual, it must be a deep spiritual cleansing to have an effect that lasts. This is the reason why God inspired me to write these books and revealed the minesweeping strategy of BIBLE CODE 7 to me, as that is the only strategy that will work. All other strategies have been tried and failed, this is guaranteed to work, it is the weaponized Word of God and comes with it's own guarantee, heaven and earth shall pass away but my Words shall not pass away, but will accomplish what I please, and I watch over my Words only, to perform them.

A housecleaning list for African Americans to be done with fasting praying and coding, BIBLE CODE 7;

Black on black murders with drugs being the common factor.

Black obesity, and self destructive nutritional lifestyle.

Black sexual promiscuity, teenage pregnancy with the result of fatherless children, child rearing Mortality and morality.

Black backsliding from the Word of God. (Hos. 4-6) and placing other things to substitute the Word.

These generational demons can only be dealt with through BIBLE CODE 7.

A rigged and stacked deck of racial injustices, stacked all the way to the Supreme Court that gives the Nine members of the Supreme Aristocracy that rules America for the ultra rich Davos Gang, and Bankers of Basel power and IMMUNITY to keep and maintain the status quo, while all the other members of the masses fight and devour each other black and white and every color in between for a fistful of dollars.

Selectively CODED to kill?

Race based DNA killers, Age specific virus killers here now?

In 1978 after I purchased my home, my lawn was in a horrendous condition with many varieties of weeds and grass, so I went to my neighbor and asked advice because his lawn was immaculate. He introduced me to a weed and feed killer product which surely did kill all varieties of the weeds, but boosted the grass's growth tremendously. I began to reason to myself, that many varieties of weeds and vegetation was killed but the grass was not. This was a powerfully selective weed killer product that went to the very DNA. From that time till now, much more powerful DNA based killer products, ingestible liquids and solids have been brought on stream to kill, maim, cripple people of certain races or color. I wrote earlier that Covid 19 is displaying the same behavior as a nano medical robot virus, a nano bot, selectively coded to kill it's victims.

The major Corporations that control the Media and their narratives are making sure that this information does not get traction in the news cycle.

The satanic globalists have a wicked plan to depopulate people of color, but Jesus Has a better one. That plan is for His Church to become muscular in spiritual Word warfare, not owning the battle, as the battle belongs to the Lord, but owning the mine sweeping strategy of BIBLE CODE 7 and victory, because He has won it for us.

Slavery seems like it might have changed, from a chattel type slavery of a bygone era, but not gone, for the demons of slavery are very much with us till today through the Constitution and the multi generational demons. Also the slavery has shape shifted to unlawful arrests, profit prisons, prison slave labor and prison criminal records.

The justice departments, Local and State Attorney Generals are rife with corruption, secret societies insider justice. Police departments are profit driven and so are these departments driven to have full prisons, yes the key driver is profits, so slavery has not ended but morphed into this dollar driven monster. How can this monster be tamed and made to heel and bow? Through BIBLE CODE 7, the minesweeping strategy of using, weaponizing the living Word of God, giving Him the battle to fight for His righteous children. There is no other way out of this rigged system of slavery-bondage.

Spiritual warfare violence with fasting through BIBLE CODE 7 is the only way, never physical violence.

Chapter 6

Stay Focused On Final Destination Jesus, Bible Code 7 Will Take You There.

The final solution and destination that needs to be sought after is not a place here on earth, neither in heaven. The final destination that all mankind should seek after is **the man Jesus Christ**. As long as we have found Him, and are following Him, we can declare to the world that we have arrived, we need to follow Him as He is the good Shepherd and we the sheep, shepherds lead and feed sheep. As long as we follow Jesus, He will lead us to heaven and everlasting life, that place where we cannot access by ourselves as Jesus is the only hope and way. Worry not about anything else here on earth, as when you have found destination Jesus you have arrived, you have found everything, that pearl of great price, sell everything and get Him. After arriving make sure you worship Jesus only and Him shall you serve. This was Jesus's instruction to the rich young ruler, follow ME Jesus commands;

Good News Translation

Jesus said to him, "If you want to be perfect, go and sell all you have and give the money to the poor, and you will have riches in heaven; then come and follow me."

***Following Jesus which means worshipping, praising, serving, living for Him is all that really matters. Store up some treasures in heaven by giving to the poor and needy yes.

Following Jesus means living a life of no regrets, heaven will be worth it all for throwing aside all earthly pleasures and sin for a season to gain the final destination, Jesus. Ponder if you will the thief on the cross, he was an evil man, a wicked murderer, who he confessed got what they deserved, death. But he found at the very last minute everything that he was searching for all his life, his final destination, then he embraced and acknowledged that destination, the person of Jesus, threw himself upon His mercy and was immediately received, embraced by Jesus. Jesus his final destination, now informed the thief that He would take him with Him to another destination called Paradise, because Jesus is the only way and leader to get there.

Will you go to Paradise? How will you get there? There is no other way but through Jesus Christ.

There is much talk about following the nation where Jesus came to, Israel, and for the saints of God to watch Israel. This is foolish and absurd evil speaking as doing so means taking focus away from the person of Jesus Christ and losing focus on our final destination, we will miss out on salvation because we miss Jesus. We must at all costs keep our eyes on Jesus and follow and serve Him only. Israel will dive into the sewer as all they that have rejected Jesus as their Messiah. Look what they will become the Bible says;

Revelation 11:8

8 And their dead bodies shall lie in the street of the great city, which spiritually is called Sodom and Egypt, where also our Lord was crucified

***Tel Aviv Israel is the most gay friendly city on planet earth, yes land of the Prophets and the Bible scriptures. Satan has perverted and corrupted it because their eyes were not on Jesus, they flat out rejected Him.

Jesus humbled himself and suffered the utmost humiliation in every way possible, He was spat upon, slapped about, mocked, whipped, tortured, and crucified naked before all to see so you and I would not be humiliated in the same manner. He took my shame upon Himself so I would not have to bear it. I am never ashamed of His name.

Isaiah 55:10-11

10 For as the rain cometh down, and the snow from heaven, and returneth not thither, but watereth the earth, and maketh it bring forth and bud, that it may give seed to the sower, and bread to the eater:
11 So shall my word be that goeth forth out of my mouth: it shall not return unto me void, but it shall accomplish that which I please, and it shall prosper in the thing whereto I sent it.

IS DESTINATION JESUS EVER COMING BACK?
WHEN WILL HE RETURN?
WHAT SIGNS DO I LOOK FOR?
2 Peter 3:8

8 But, beloved, be not ignorant of this one thing, that one day is with the Lord as a thousand years, and a thousand years as one day.

Matthew the tax collector, was a Jew who embraced Jesus and became a disciple. Matthew's message was very concise and was primarily for the Jewish people.

John wrote in a manner and style which was primarily directed to the Church, all who would believe on Jesus Christ.

Mark was not a disciple of Jesus and his book was written primarily to the Romans, very terse, to the point and concise.

Dr. Luke, he stipulates, was an investigative reporter who researched all evidence and data about Jesus and placed it in a concise <u>order</u>, true of a great investigative reporter. (Luke 1 vs.1-4)

Jesus now gives a chronology of events to be manifested in the future
Matthew 24:15-31

15 When ye therefore shall see the abomination of desolation, spoken of by Daniel the prophet, stand in the holy place, (whoso readeth, let him understand:)

***The legalization of sodomy and lesbianism in place of holy matrimony. The abomination that causes God to lay waste and make desolate all nations that practice these wicked Babylonian abominations.

16 Then let them which be in Judaea flee into the mountains:
17 Let him which is on the housetop not come down to take any thing out of his house:

201

18 Neither let him which is in the field return back to take his clothes.

19 And woe unto them that are with child, and to them that give suck in those days!

20 But pray ye that your flight be not in the winter, neither on the sabbath day:

After 2016's approval of sodomy in the USA, Christians should have begun to flee Babylon. However God did not begin to reveal to me His Word and plans until October 2017 when I started to write my first book "The Hundredfold".

21 For then shall be great tribulation, such as was not since the beginning of the world to this time, no, nor ever shall be.

22 And except those days should be shortened, there should no flesh be saved: but for the elect's sake those days shall be shortened.

***The entrance into this great tribulation era has begun with Covid 19, never since the world began have we ever seen such great tribulation, distress worldwide all at once. The Agenda has begun, twenty five percent of the world's population will soon die quickly. (Revelation 6 vs.8)

23 Then if any man shall say unto you, Lo, here is Christ, or there; believe it not.

24 For there shall arise false Christs, and false prophets, and shall shew great signs and wonders; insomuch that, if it were possible, they shall deceive the very elect.

25 Behold, I have told you before.

26 Wherefore if they shall say unto you, Behold, he is in the desert; go not forth: behold, he is in the secret chambers; believe it not.

27 For as the lightning cometh out of the east, and shineth even unto the west; so shall also the coming of the Son of man be.

28 For wheresoever the carcase is, there will the eagles be gathered together.

***7 Seals Judgements

Just about this time the **7 seals Judgements** shall begin. The Four Horsemen of the Apocalypse, (The Revealing or Revelation) will begin to ride concurrently. No one knows for sure if these judgements will be in chronological order as written in the Bible.

First seal Judgement–The White Horse. Conquering, false religions.

Second seal Judgement–The Red Horse. Wars and men killing each other on earth.

Third seal Judgement–The Black Horse. Expensive food prices, a loaf of bread for a days wage.

Fourth seal Judgement–The Pale Horse. Death followed by hell, **25%** of the world's population, **two billion people,** will die from famines, wars, diseases and beasts of the field.

The Fifth seal Judgement–Martyrs for faith in Jesus and holding the testimony of Jesus, the souls under the Altar of God told to wait a little while longer until their brethren that should be killed in like manner are killed also.

29 Immediately after the tribulation of those days shall the sun be darkened, and the moon shall not give

her light, and the stars shall fall from heaven, and the powers of the heavens shall be shaken:

The sixth seal judgement.

***So following hard on the heels of the great tribulation is another frightful catastrophe, the day of The Lord, a horror of great dread.

This is definitely the **Sixth seal Judgement** upon the earth, or **the day of the Lord I believe.** Every Bible reference to the day of the Lord refers to the sun turning black and the moon blood red with the stars of heaven falling. All men bar none, will run to the hills, caves and dens and cry out, "fall on us and hide us from Him who sits on the throne". This earthquake is so massive that Islands and mountains move out of their places. How many will die or be displaced by this? Billions. Satan's fury is overrun by God's mightier fury.

Seventh seal Judgement begins–silence in heaven for half an hour. A scene of impending doom and destruction is about to happen. The angel lines up 7 other angels with 7 trumpets that are ready to sound one after the other, but first that angel places incense on live coals and sends this beautiful aroma of burning incense up to The Lord along with the prayers of the saints of God. He then takes live hot coals, places it in his censer and pours it out upon the earth and there is hail, fire, and blood coming down from heaven upon the earth upon all mankind.

The One Third Judgements or 7 Trumpets Judgements.

This Judgements is upon all mankind who followed satan and his evil angels, one third of which rebelled against The Lord and were cast out of eternity into time upon earth with satan.

First Trumpet Judgement–The trumpet sounds and fire comes down from heaven and burns up one third of the trees, one third of all green grass is destroyed, burned.

The second Trumpet Judgement–A great mountain burning with fire was cast into the sea, and a third part of the sea became blood, a third part of the sea creatures died and a third part of the ships, boats were destroyed. (Not mentioned was the huge Tsunami created and that most cities will be inundated, and all city and coastal dwellers will be killed by this horrendous tsunami.

The third Trumpet Judgement–A huge star named Wormwood now falls from heaven, it is fragmented and falls upon the rivers and springs of water making it bitter and non potable and many people died from drinking bitter, non potable, poisoned waters.

The fourth Trumpet Judgement–one third part of the sun, moon and stars are hidden and refuse to give light like a blackout or dim-out. One third of the day was therefore without light. The cause, not revealed here, but it will come to pass. This will be the second time.

The fifth Trumpet Judgement–A star (God's mighty Angel) fell from heaven being given the key of the bottomless pit and commanded to open it. Intelligent locust shaped entities came out of the pit and was given the command to hurt for five months, give a very painful sting to all mankind who did **not have God's seal in their foreheads**. The sealed, chosen ones of Jesus are protected by Him always.

Their sting was like that of a scorpion with the pain of it like a scorpion. All mankind who do not have God's seal upon their foreheads will be stung, and beg to die because of the great pain, but death will not come to them, they will still live even if they try to blow their brains out with a gun, or jump off a

205

tall building, there will be no death. Have you seen the recent zombie movies coming out? The walking dead with body parts hanging off them, but still alive, well here it is, very real about to happen, coming soon to planet earth. A movie scripted from the Bible, so real and about to be revealed world wide, be ready get Jesus's mark and become immune from this. The name of the leader of these locust entities has the name Apollyon, or Abaddon.

The sixth Trumpet Judgement–This angel was told to loose the four angels bound in the River Euphrates. These four angels had a mandate to kill one third, 33% of all mankind left upon the earth in warfare. A 200 million man army is now mustered, a fight results among nations and armies, resulting in the mass death of 33% of all mankind. So let's calculate, 2 billion dead previously, now of the six billion left, 33% or 2 billion more dies, so we have a combined 4 billion dead plus those other collateral damages, so about four and a half billion are now dead out of eight billion, leaving approximately three and a half billion people on planet earth. The world's population is now more than halved. Where are all these people buried? And how quickly? Will there be a spread of diseases because of dogs and other animals eating human bodies, proliferating, multiplying and spreading the diseases like wildfire? Will there be enough sane, healthy strong people left to bury the dead? Will there still be air, sea, Road travel?

Still after all this there is no repentance from men, they continued in all sinful ways and deeds. Neither is there any repentance from their sorceries.

The seven Thunders Judgement–The Lord instructed John not to reveal it. For his ears and eyes only.

THE RAPTURE IS NOW ABOUT TO HAPPEN

**"There shall be time no longer,
It's over, or the end of the age has now come."
The 7th or LAST Trumpet Judgement–
The Last Trump is about to sound.
A POWERFUL SHIFT IS NOW ABOUT TO HAPPEN!**

Revelation 10:7

7 But in the days of the voice of the seventh angel, when he shall begin to sound, the mystery of God should be finished, as he hath declared to his servants the prophets.

Revelation 11:15-19

15 And the seventh angel sounded; and there were great voices in heaven, saying, The kingdoms of this world are become the kingdoms of our Lord, and of his Christ; and he shall reign for ever and ever.

16 And the four and twenty elders, which sat before God on their seats, fell upon their faces, and worshipped God,

17 Saying, We give thee thanks, O Lord God Almighty, which art, and wast, and art to come; because thou hast taken to thee thy great power, and hast reigned.

18 And the nations were angry, and thy wrath is come, and the time of the dead, that they should be judged, and that thou shouldest give reward unto thy servants the prophets, and to the saints, and them that fear thy name, small and great; and shouldest destroy them which destroy the earth.

19 And the temple of God was opened in heaven, and there was seen in his temple the ark of his testament: and there were lightnings, and voices, and thunderings, and an earthquake, and great hail.

1 Corinthians 15:51-53

51 Behold, I shew you a mystery; We shall not all sleep, but we shall all be changed,

52 In a moment, in the twinkling of an eye, at the last trump: for the trumpet shall sound, and the dead shall be raised incorruptible, and we shall be changed.

53 For this corruptible must put on incorruption, and this mortal must put on immortality.

Revelation 14:14-16

14 And I looked, and behold a white cloud, and upon the cloud one sat like unto the Son of man, having on his head a golden crown, and in his hand a sharp sickle.

15 And another angel came out of the temple, crying with a loud voice to him that sat on the cloud, Thrust in thy sickle, and reap: for the time is come for thee to reap; for the harvest of the earth is ripe.

16 And he that sat on the cloud thrust in his sickle on the earth; and the earth was reaped.

Matthew 24

30 And then shall appear the sign of the Son of man in heaven: and then shall all the tribes of the earth mourn, and they shall see the Son of man coming in the clouds of heaven with power and great glory.

31 And he shall send his angels with a great sound of a trumpet, and they shall gather together his elect from the four winds, from one end of heaven to the other.

***Now comes what all Christians have been told about would happen before the great tribulation time, the RAPTURE. It occurs when the Bible says it would after the **last trumpet,**

the 7th trumpet. Now just as the Bible reveals here we are not to be in darkness, deception, under the influence of satan when it comes to the Word of God as we are children of light, not of darkness. Our duty is to watch and be sober, be in constant Word warfare prayers so satan cannot deceive by his clouds of darkness.

1 Thessalonians 5:4-6

4 But ye, brethren, are not in darkness, that that day should overtake you as a thief.

5 Ye are all the children of light, and the children of the day: we are not of the night, nor of darkness.

6 Therefore let us not sleep, as do others; but let us watch and be sober.

***This is the mechanics of Jesus's return to earth to receive His bride Himself, the dead in Him rising from their graves first then afterwards those who are living and have maintained faith in Him. Jesus our final destination, now takes us to to His destination Paradise to be with Him for all eternity;

1 Thessalonians 4:16-18

16 For the Lord himself shall descend from heaven with a shout, with the voice of the archangel, and with the trump of God: and the dead in Christ shall rise first:

17 Then we which are alive and remain shall be caught up together with them in the clouds, to meet the Lord in the air: and so shall we ever be with the Lord.

18 Wherefore comfort one another with these words.

<u>Show me God Almighty, who is He that I may know Him?</u>

See Jesus, and see God Almighty.

A discourse with the disciples to which Jesus cautioned His disciples to stop trying to go above His head and authority in seeking the Father. Jesus confronts His disciples and warns them to consistently seek Him and not God, as seeing Him equates to seeing God, and God cannot be seen or encountered without Him, Jesus.

He further warns His disciples to do the great works because of Him, and that God who is enmeshed in Him will manifest the mighty works. All asking of or from God must be done in the name of Jesus Christ only, no other name but His. So guys, go for it, ask in my name, it shall be done for you.

John 14:8-14

8 Philip saith unto him, Lord, shew us the Father, and it sufficeth us.

9 Jesus saith unto him, Have I been so long time with you, and yet hast thou not known me, Philip? he that hath seen me hath seen the Father; and how sayest thou then, Shew us the Father?

10 Believest thou not that I am in the Father, and the Father in me? the words that I speak unto you I speak not of myself: but the Father that dwelleth in me, he doeth the works.

11 Believe me that I am in the Father, and the Father in me: or else believe me for the very works' sake.

12 Verily, verily, I say unto you, He that believeth on me, the works that I do shall he do also; and greater works than these shall he do; because I go unto my Father.

13 And whatsoever ye shall ask in my name, that will I do, that the Father may be glorified in the Son.

14 If ye shall ask any thing in my name, I will do it.

Chapter 7

Coding The Judgement Strikes For Self Defense And Preservation.

CODING = declaring the scripture audibly 7 Times or more per day.

Not if, but when the enemy gets in your face, stand your ground, resist the devil and make him flee from you, shout boldly, "**I plead the blood of Jesus Christ against you**" **(repeatedly). Terrorize them that would terrorize you.** Rain down the fire of God's Word upon them and watch them take off running like madmen. But stand your ground at all costs, don't run, don't cower in fear, but fight with the Word of God, and the BLOOD OF JESUS. They must run from you in fear. No more backing down, no more being nice, it's war, it's a spiritual brawl now and you've been declared the winner, but you must respond. No response = death.

King David conquered territories, consolidated, expanded and ruled the new larger Israel for forty years, of which he suffered many hostilities, difficulties and strife, but for a great reason. He warred a great warfare, both physically and spiritually, and he proved and mastered the art of spiritual warfare through BIBLE CODE 7. David, the man after God's own heart, wrote 76 Psalms, in the Book of Psalms, no other book. These Psalms are very powerful and a testimony of David overcoming **all** his adversaries who sought to kill him. He defeated them all and reigned forty years. After this, he gave his son Solomon the KEYS, the scriptures he wrote, advised him sternly of the blessings and benefits of these imprecatory Psalms that the Holy Spirit gave him at his lowest moments in life and advised Solomon to use them always. Be always on the offensive, don't wait for something to happen, but go offensive spiritual warfare at all times. This was his advised battle strategy given to Solomon. Just like his father, Solomon sought understanding with discernment from The Lord and received it. Solomon now began to reign over all Israel and ruled for forty years, but there was a very strange difference in his reign. No one lifted a finger to attack or harm him or the kingdom of Israel, none. Forty years of peaceful reign, why?

The answer is found in this verse of scripture Psalm 17, attributed to the writings of Solomon, in addition to the Books of Ecclesiastes, Proverbs, Songs of Solomon, here;

Psalm 17:4-5

4 Concerning the works of men, by the word of thy lips
I have kept me from the paths of the destroyer.
5 Hold up my goings in thy paths, that my footsteps slip not.

Solomon used the spiritual nuclear option of God's Word, BIBLE CODE 7, violent, offensive, spiritual warfare to achieve forty years of peaceful reign over all Israel, and not one enemy rose up against him.

If it worked for Kings David, Solomon, for me, it will work for you also.

No one can hide from the presence of God.
We can however hide in the presence of God,

To conclude, this diabolical plot to destroy millions, in utilizing a race specific, age specific remote controlled nano robotic killer virus, a nano medical invisible virus that has been turned loose upon the world to terminate millions of people from the earth, so the earth can be sustainably managed and developed. What will God's response be? God will strike the very seat, top tier rulers of the ruling class wicked rich that rules over the poor. A surgical strike will be made from the Righteous Judge, The Lord Himself, you can depend on it, here is His Word of promise;

Revelation 16:10-11

10 And the fifth angel poured out his vial upon the seat of the beast; and his kingdom was full of darkness; and they gnawed their tongues for pain,

11 And blasphemed the God of heaven because of their pains and their sores, and repented not of their deeds.

In the meanwhile, God will respond with His own unstoppable viruses, His plagues will be sent to terminate the terminators. Twenty one judgement strikes will be made But for His children to stay secure, they must be hidden in Him, through His Word;

Psalm 119 vs. 164

Seven times a day I have given praise to thee, for the judgments of thy justice.

The declaring of God's Words 7 Times brings into manifestation the judgement hand of God to do mighty miracles on your behalf. I have outlined this in all my previous books especially my first book, "The Hundredfold through BIBLE CODE 7". (Get a copy and study) These scriptures are only some of the judgement scriptures against the wicked deceitful adversaries.

So make sure you draw near to Jesus first, then resist the devil and make him run from you in terror Through BIBLE CODE 7.

The walls of Jericho would not come down with six trips around it, it had to be 7.

Naaman would not be healed with six dips in river Jordan, it needed 7 dips.

Prophet Elijah spoke judgement upon Israel once, but would not have gotten the rains of blessings to reverse it if he had only prayed six times, it took 7 Times.

So let's go begin to CODE these scriptures, as many scriptures as you choose 7 times and see the powerful results.

Psalm 149:6-9

6 Let the high praises of God be in their mouth, and a twoedged sword in their hand;

7 To execute vengeance upon the heathen, and punishments upon the people;

8 To bind their kings with chains, and their nobles with fetters of iron;

9 To execute upon them the judgment written: this honour have all his saints. Praise ye the Lord.

Isaiah 41:10-14

10 Fear thou not; for I am with thee: be not dismayed; for I am thy God: I will strengthen thee; yea, I will help thee; yea, I will uphold thee with the right hand of my righteousness.

11 Behold, all they that were incensed against thee shall be ashamed and confounded: they shall be as nothing; and they that strive with thee shall perish.

12 Thou shalt seek them, and shalt not find them, even them that contended with thee: they that war against thee shall be as nothing, and as a thing of nought.

13 For I the Lord thy God will hold thy right hand, saying unto thee, Fear not; I will help thee.

14 Fear not, thou worm Jacob, and ye men of Israel; I will help thee, saith the Lord, and thy redeemer, the Holy One of Israel.

Isaiah 51:7-12

7 Hearken unto me, ye that know righteousness, the people in whose heart is my law; fear ye not the reproach of men, neither be ye afraid of their revilings.

8 For the moth shall eat them up like a garment, and the worm shall eat them like wool: but my righteousness shall be for ever, and my salvation from generation to generation.

9 Awake, awake, put on strength, O arm of the Lord; awake, as in the ancient days, in the generations of old. Art thou not it that hath cut Rahab, and wounded the dragon?

10 Art thou not it which hath dried the sea, the waters of the great deep; that hath made the depths of the sea a way for the ransomed to pass over?

11 Therefore the redeemed of the Lord shall return, and come with singing unto Zion; and everlasting joy shall be upon their head: they shall obtain gladness and joy; and sorrow and mourning shall flee away.

12 I, even I, am he that comforteth you: who art thou, that thou shouldest be afraid of a man that shall die, and of the son of man which shall be made as grass;

Isaiah 51:21-23

21 Therefore hear now this, thou afflicted, and drunken, but not with wine:

22 Thus saith thy Lord the Lord, and thy God that pleadeth the cause of his people, Behold, I have taken out of thine hand the cup of trembling, even the dregs of the cup of my fury; thou shalt no more drink it again:

23 But I will put it into the hand of them that afflict thee; which have said to thy soul, Bow down, that we may go over: and thou hast laid thy body as the ground, and as the street, to them that went over.

Isaiah 54:17

17 No weapon that is formed against thee shall prosper; and every tongue that shall rise against thee in judgment thou shalt condemn. This is the heritage of the servants of the Lord, and their righteousness is of me, saith the Lord.

Isaiah 49:24-26

24 Shall the prey be taken from the mighty, or the lawful captive delivered?

25 But thus saith the Lord, Even the captives of the mighty shall be taken away, and the prey of the terrible

shall be delivered: for I will contend with him that contendeth with thee, and I will save thy children.

26 And I will feed them that oppress thee with their own flesh; and they shall be drunken with their own blood, as with sweet wine: and all flesh shall know that I the Lord am thy Saviour and thy Redeemer, the mighty One of Jacob.

Psalm 83:9-18

9 Do unto them as unto the Midianites; as to Sisera, as to Jabin, at the brook of Kison:

10 Which perished at Endor: they became as dung for the earth.

11 Make their nobles like Oreb, and like Zeeb: yea, all their princes as Zebah, and as Zalmunna:

12 Who said, Let us take to ourselves the houses of God in possession.

13 O my God, make them like a wheel; as the stubble before the wind.

14 As the fire burneth a wood, and as the flame setteth the mountains on fire;

15 So persecute them with thy tempest, and make them afraid with thy storm.

16 Fill their faces with shame; that they may seek thy name, O Lord.

17 Let them be confounded and troubled for ever; yea, let them be put to shame, and perish:

18 That men may know that thou, whose name alone is Jehovah, art the most high over all the earth.

Psalm 69:22-28

22 Let their table become a snare before them: and that which should have been for their welfare, let it become a trap.

23 Let their eyes be darkened, that they see not; and make their loins continually to shake.

24 Pour out thine indignation upon them, and let thy wrathful anger take hold of them.

25 Let their habitation be desolate; and let none dwell in their tents.

26 For they persecute him whom thou hast smitten; and they talk to the grief of those whom thou hast wounded.

27 Add iniquity unto their iniquity: and let them not come into thy righteousness.

28 Let them be blotted out of the book of the living, and not be written with the righteous.

Psalm 109:11-20

11 Let the extortioner catch all that he hath; and let the strangers spoil his labour.

12 Let there be none to extend mercy unto him: neither let there be any to favour his fatherless children.

13 Let his posterity be cut off; and in the generation following let their name be blotted out.

14 Let the iniquity of his fathers be remembered with the Lord; and let not the sin of his mother be blotted out.

15 Let them be before the Lord continually, that he may cut off the memory of them from the earth.

16 Because that he remembered not to shew mercy, but persecuted the poor and needy man, that he might even slay the broken in heart.

17 As he loved cursing, so let it come unto him: as he delighted not in blessing, so let it be far from him.

18 As he clothed himself with cursing like as with his garment, so let it come into his bowels like water, and like oil into his bones.

19 Let it be unto him as the garment which covereth him, and for a girdle wherewith he is girded continually.

20 Let this be the reward of mine adversaries from the Lord, and of them that speak evil against my soul.

Deuteronomy 32:41-43

41 If I whet my glittering sword, and mine hand take hold on judgment; I will render vengeance to mine enemies, and will reward them that hate me.

42 I will make mine arrows drunk with blood, and my sword shall devour flesh; and that with the blood of the slain and of the captives, from the beginning of revenges upon the enemy.

43 Rejoice, O ye nations, with his people: for he will avenge the blood of his servants, and will render vengeance to his adversaries, and will be merciful unto his land, and to his people.

Nahum 1:2

2 God is jealous, and the Lord revengeth; the Lord revengeth, and is furious; the Lord will take vengeance on his adversaries, and he reserveth wrath for his enemies.

Job 20:4-19

4 Knowest thou not this of old, since man was placed upon earth,

5 That the triumphing of the wicked is short, and the joy of the hypocrite but for a moment?

6 Though his excellency mount up to the heavens, and his head reach unto the clouds;

7 Yet he shall perish for ever like his own dung: they which have seen him shall say, Where is he?

8 He shall fly away as a dream, and shall not be found: yea, he shall be chased away as a vision of the night.

9 The eye also which saw him shall see him no more; neither shall his place any more behold him.

10 His children shall seek to please the poor, and his hands shall restore their goods.

11 His bones are full of the sin of his youth, which shall lie down with him in the dust.

12 Though wickedness be sweet in his mouth, though he hide it under his tongue;

13 Though he spare it, and forsake it not; but keep it still within his mouth:

14 Yet his meat in his bowels is turned, it is the gall of asps within him.

15 He hath swallowed down riches, and he shall vomit them up again: God shall cast them out of his belly.

16 He shall suck the poison of asps: the viper's tongue shall slay him.

17 He shall not see the rivers, the floods, the brooks of honey and butter.

18 That which he laboured for shall he restore, and shall not swallow it down: according to his substance shall the restitution be, and he shall not rejoice therein.

19 Because he hath oppressed and hath forsaken the poor; because he hath violently taken away an house which he builded not;

Proverbs 13:22

22 A good man leaveth an inheritance to his children's children: and the wealth of the sinner is laid up for the just.

1 Kings 21:23-24

23 And of Jezebel also spake the Lord, saying, The dogs shall eat Jezebel by the wall of Jezreel.

24 Him that dieth of Ahab in the city the dogs shall eat; and him that dieth in the field shall the fowls of the air eat.

1 Kings 21:29

29 Seest thou how Ahab humbleth himself before me? because he humbleth himself before me, I will not bring the evil in his days: but in his son's days will I bring the evil upon his house.

Psalm 55:22-23

22 Cast thy burden upon the Lord, and he shall sustain thee: he shall never suffer the righteous to be moved.

23 But thou, O God, shalt bring them down into the pit of destruction: bloody and deceitful men shall not live out half their days; but I will trust in thee.

Psalm 5:6

6 Thou shalt destroy them that speak leasing: the Lord will abhor the bloody and deceitful man.

Psalm 139:19

19 Surely thou wilt slay the wicked, O God: depart from me therefore, ye bloody men.

Proverbs 24:20

20 For there shall be no reward to the evil man; the candle of the wicked shall be put out.

Psalm 55:15

15 Let death seize upon them, and let them go down quick into hell: for wickedness is in their dwellings, and among them.

Deuteronomy 28:20

20 The Lord shall send upon thee cursing, vexation, and rebuke, in all that thou settest thine hand unto for to do, until thou be destroyed, and until thou perish quickly; because of the wickedness of thy doings, whereby thou hast forsaken me.

Psalm 68:2

2 As smoke is driven away, so drive them away: as wax melteth before the fire, so let the wicked perish at the presence of God.

Proverbs 28:28

28 When the wicked rise, men hide themselves: but when they perish, the righteous increase.

Ecclesiastes 7:15

15 All things have I seen in the days of my vanity: there is a just man that perisheth in his righteousness, and there is a wicked man that prolongeth his life in his wickedness.

Psalm 37:20

20 But the wicked shall perish, and the enemies of the Lord shall be as the fat of lambs: they shall consume; into smoke shall they consume away.

Psalm 140:11

11 Let not an evil speaker be established in the earth: evil shall hunt the violent man to overthrow him.

Acts 19:15-20

15 And the evil spirit answered and said, Jesus I know, and Paul I know; but who are ye?

16 And the man in whom the evil spirit was leaped on them, and overcame them, and prevailed against them, so that they fled out of that house naked and wounded.

17 And this was known to all the Jews and Greeks also dwelling at Ephesus; and fear fell on them all, and the name of the Lord Jesus was magnified.

18 And many that believed came, and confessed, and shewed their deeds.

19 Many of them also which used curious arts brought their books together, and burned them before all men: and they counted the price of them, and found it fifty thousand pieces of silver.

20 So mightily grew the word of God and prevailed.

***Jesus warned us that the Church that received the best commendation from Him, the Philadelphia Church, had a sworn secretive, lying, inside Judas enemy that they were not familiar with, the Synagogue of satan, but Jesus will make them worship before our feet;

Revelation 3

8I know thy works: behold, I have set before thee an open door, and no man can shut it: for thou hast a little strength, and hast kept my word, and hast not denied my name. 9Behold, I will make them of the synagogue of Satan, which say they are Jews, and are not, but do lie; behold, I will make them to come and worship before thy feet, and to know that I have loved thee. 10Because thou hast kept the word of my patience, I also will keep thee from the hour of temptation, which shall come upon all the world, to try them that dwell upon the earth.

The **WORD** of God is the Lord Jesus, every knee must bow to Him and confess Him as Lord of all, the **BOSS** of all bosses. Jesus mentions the keeping of His Word and not denying His name, here in this passage of scripture. It is important to know that The day is now here where Local Governments and private corporations are asking employees for the voluntary taking of a chip inserted in the hand for I.D. and access purposes.

Let's see the prayer of Jeremiah as he calls upon The Lord to vindicate him from his inside enemies, his own people who were setting traps for him to kill him, but note what they said about the teachings of the priests, and words of the prophets which are the Words of God that these Words will never disappear, they will surely stand as God watches over them to confirm these Words;

Jeremiah 18

18Then they said, "Let's plot against Jeremiah, because the teachings of the priests, the advice of wise people,

and the word of the prophets won't disappear. Accuse
him! Pay no attention to anything he says."
19Pay attention to me, O LORD, and listen to what my
accusers say.
20Good should not be paid back with evil. They dig a
pit to take my life. Remember how I stood in your presence and pleaded for them in order to turn your anger
away from them.
21Now, hand their children over to famine. Pour out
their [blood] by using your sword. Then their wives will
become childless widows. Their husbands will be put to
death. Their young men will be struck down in battle.
22Make them cry out from their homes when you suddenly send troops against them, because they dug a pit
to catch me and hid snares for my feet.
23But you, O LORD, know that they plan to kill me.
Don't forgive their crimes. Don't wipe their sins out of
your sight. Make them stumble in your presence. Deal
with them when you get angry.

***Jeremiah's request to The Lord, whatever they sow, let
them also reap. Vengeance belongs to you O my God, so let me
see your vengeance upon my enemies that seek my very life, I
am your son, they are not, save and defend me and my very life
from them, I shall live and not die and declare your wonderful
works, so vindicate me o Lord.

The Lord, the avenger will destroy your enemies, the
assembly of the wicked and deceitful that seeks to kill you
and your families, let Him go to work for you by reminding
Him of His Words which is the strategy of BIBLE CODE 7,
self preservation and defense. There is no better Judge, killer,
defender, protector, preserver than Jesus, He's on duty 24/7. So

why would you not desire Him to work for you? All you have to do is surrender your whole life to Him, trust Him call upon Him with His sworn promises, His Words and see Him begin to move mightily. Your angels need no sleep or coffee breaks, so you do the recitals, declaring of His Words and let Him do the fighting, the battle is not yours, but His.

Directed energy weapons, laser weapons will be used to fight wars now.
Increase in use of DEWs to reduce military operational cost as well as enhance military capabilities. (Source; army-technology.com)

With the use of DEWs, military forces will be able to modify the weapon based on situational requirements, which will help to reduce operational costs. Furthermore, as the DEWs can be launched using platform generated power, it will require no additional cost of ammunition. This factor will lead to a further reduction in military operational costs and enhance the defensive and offensive capabilities of the armed forces.

Global warfare is rapidly evolving. Threats are becoming more sophisticated and technologically advanced. Using expensive single-use missiles to eliminate small targets such as drones and swarm boats is not a sustainable strategy. Directed energy weapons offer huge potential cost savings in various tactical scenarios. Traditional weapons cost thousands or millions of dollars per shot and are limited by availability.

According to the US DoD and US Navy, the cost per shot of a laser weapon is estimated to be $1. This factor has driven more investment into the global DEWs market. Demand for such systems by military forces is expected to increase.

Is this prophecied biblically? Yes it sure is. Why is it important that we are aware of this weaponry?

Zechariah 14:12

12 And this shall be the plague wherewith the Lord will smite all the people that have fought against Jerusalem; Their flesh shall consume away while they stand upon their feet, and their eyes shall consume away in their holes, and their tongue shall consume away in their mouth.

In the book of Revelation, we read of the beast calling down fire from heaven, that will be used as a threat also, if you don't worship me, I will destroy your cities, is this type of blackmail possible?

Yes it is, Worship satan, or be destroyed in a furnace of fire from heaven,

Revelation 13:13-14

13 And he doeth great wonders, so that he maketh fire come down from heaven on the earth in the sight of men, 14 And deceiveth them that dwell on the earth by the means of those miracles which he had power to do in the sight of the beast; saying to them that dwell on the earth, that they should make an image to the beast, which had the wound by a sword, and did live.

The direct energy weapons are the weapons of now, today, thereby fulfilling the Bible prophecies.

Now USA possesses all these weapons and believe that because they do, they are the most advanced nation on earth with Russia, and China. However the weaponries of God from

His Armory will be far superior and will devastate the USA many times over.

The world needs a clear vision of the future and a concise strategy of how to get there. Nothing seems to make sense anymore, it seems like the world is stumbling and groping in the dark which it is, but we as believers, however are walking in the light of Jesus knowing who and whose we are. We are not abandoned orphans, the blind of the world leads the blinded masses into a spiritual cesspool. This is reaching critical mass as there is mass bloodshed all around us. A run to the hills moment is soon approaching as the jobs of the people are not their lives.

Here's where we are going to be;
Revelation 7

13And one of the elders answered, saying unto me, What are these which are arrayed in white robes? and whence came they? 14And I said unto him, Sir, thou knowest. And he said to me, These are they which came out of great tribulation, and have washed their robes, and made them white in the blood of the Lamb. 15Therefore are they before the throne of God, and serve him day and night in his temple: and he that sitteth on the throne shall dwell among them. 16They shall hunger no more, neither thirst any more; neither shall the sun light on them, nor any heat. 17For the Lamb which is in the midst of the throne shall feed them, and shall lead them unto living fountains of waters: and God shall wipe away all tears from their eyes.

For all eternity, Amen.

A Message To Moderate, Reasonable White America, Including The Good Ole White Boys, Can We Talk?

White America, Black America, Hispanic America have been duped all along and it's time for us to be awakened from sleep to visualize the giant that we can together become. It's time for us to join forces and fight this hatred and bigotry that divides us, or the alternative will be that we will waste energy to hate one another, fight against each other and then kill one another.

White America, you are fighting against the black man who did you no wrong, did not harm you in any way, but only desires to have some of what you got in life and to live in peace. Black America was taken from Africa against their will and forced to work the plantations for 250 + years. Was indoctrinated and told they were no better than a horse or mule, chattel property. Was denied being taught to read or write, with those who broke the rule of not teaching the slaves being imprisoned for 1-12 months, was promised **40** acres and a mule per family for that hard generational **250** year labor, but was shafted and given nothing. A lying empty promise and a brutal letdown. Left in poverty and despair to lick the wounds and insults of **400** years of slavery, free labor to build this nation into an industrial powerhouse nation that it is, even until today, the black descendants of slavery trudged forward after being plundered, looted, segregated, but against all odds, and dire persecutions are still standing today.

Moderate white America, and good ole boys, your real enemy is the very rich white slave owner class that has duped you and turned you against a black man to keep you and us so busy we cant see the real enemy, we can't see for looking who the real enemy is. The oldest satanic strategy of deception is used by the rich ruling class to **DIVIDE, DIVIDE** and conquer, to rule over all those beneath them that they call the masses.

The strategy is if we can keep them fighting among themselves, they will never have time to figure out who we the real enemy is, the ones that keep them in bondage, in slavery, as black slaves and as white slaves together, only a little bit separated by money and social class, but slaves anyhow.

We'll keep the white slaves in bondage in a nice house, but by alcohol, beer, sports, credit card and mortgage debt as borrowers are slaves to the lender. Make them feel comfy as blue collar and middle class people, but slaves anyhow. We will keep the black slave descendants in bondage by sheer poverty, beer, wines, drugs, ghetto living, police discrimination with brutality. We will prey upon them both in the political party systems of Democrats and

Republicans as this is a great strategy to keep them on the political plantation, and severely divided, but we will control both political parties, so we win anyhow. White moderate slaves, black poor slaves, and white, beer drinking, good ole boy drinking slaves, they are all our slaves, fools and don't know it.

Moderate white America, white boys, open your eyes and look, get WOKE and see that you and your fellow white brothers, sisters and children are dying like flies from opioids, fentanyl, heroin, meth and all manner of drugs just like the black and Hispanic man.

Who makes that big money from the drugs that kills Whites as well as Blacks and Hispanics?

The big money dogs, the slave owners, the rich satanic ruling class.

White, Black and Hispanic young people are all dying an equal opportunity death from these scourges, so let's get real and deal with each other as victims together, like hurting brothers and sisters.

Blacks and Hispanics desire the same things you desire, to work a good job get a paycheck and feed our families, drive a decent car or pickup, start a small business, live in a decent place to call home with food on our tables and clothes on our backs. But who took the great manufacturing jobs out of America and into communist China and left us jobless and broke? Who stifled businesses in red tape, rules, regulations to frustrate keeping businesses here in America? Then who made us to fight each other for the scraps that was left and hate each other because we have different skin color, or people come from a different country and speak another language?

Let's talk, can we? There's room for us here, if you budge a little and move over a little, theres room for us, we can get along, our desires are the same and we can be a benefit and a blessing to each other. Don't be afraid of us, as we are human people just like you that will help you just as you help us.

Moderate white America, white good ole boys, we are holding out the olive branch of friendship and love to you, we are extending an invitation to you to meet us at the table, the feast table of Jesus, as no other social cement or glue can hold us together but Jesus's shed blood.

Listen carefully white America, it was your Dr. Billy Graham and many other Evangelists and Churches that brought the good news of Jesus to the Islands, Latin America, Africa and across the whole world, never Russia or china, but the USA, yes the good WHITE AMERICAN people with the love of Jesus Christ. It was white America that gave poor peoples milk powder and cheeses in USAID so millions of children all over these countries can have strong bones and teeth.

Yes white America, we remember, love and appreciate you for all this, but can you kindly budge and kick start this LOVE here in America once again? Can you begin by reaching across the aisle to us as we reach out to you? Can you please try to reach out to some countries and peoples around and about you to bridge the love gap, and destroy the hate bridge? Please America, let's try, and as we try, Jesus will meet us in the middle. Let me make it loud and abundantly clear,

"We love you moderate white America, good ole white boys, with the love of Jesus Christ."

BLM and Antifa does not represent the masses of African Americans or other nationalities that is in the real America.

Jesus Christ alone can erase satan's demons of hate and division that makes us hate and fight one another, and will bring us to turn around together and fight the common enemy that has caused us to fight each other for too long. That enemy is the satanic rich, the anti-Jesus people, I have labelled them the "TEN PERCENTERS".

Do you really know and understand why you hate us?

Why you fight against us?

Because of the slave owners, the elites, the ruling class, the very satanic rich Ten Percenters" who own and control 85% of the world's wealth, while we the masses, 90%, fight and destroy each other for the other 15% of the world's wealth. These are they whose table you could not sit at and dine with them, has fed you lies for too long to keep us as they refer to us as, the masses, the poor, the downtrodden. Their strategy is to keep us busy, divided, being envious, jealous, fighting and hating each other. Divide and rule over them, they say. We have been so busy fighting and hating each other, we never had time to look and see who the real enemy is, the "Ten Percenters".

If you can't say amen with me on this, then you need to check your Jesus temperature, see if you're hot or cold, check your Jesus meter to see if you're on or off, full or empty. You need to check your Jesus altimeter to see if you're on top or flying near the bottom, ascending or descending as without Jesus you are a fool, and like putty in the hands of satan as he takes you and turns you any which way he desires but loose.

Galatians 3:28

28 There is neither Jew nor Greek, there is neither bond nor free, there is neither male nor female: for ye are all one in Christ Jesus.

So lets wake up and smell the coffee, we the "masses", moderate whites, good ole boys, blacks, Hispanics are fighting each other when we should be gathered to fight the real enemy, the satanic ruling class 'ten percenters', not with guns and bullets, murders and beatings, looting and shooting but by weaponizing the Word of God, BIBLE CODE 7, the real guns and bullets, the spiritual nuclear option of God that can never fail and assail the wicked, for God is angry with the wicked every day.

So let's throw off the yoke of oppression and deceit and dive into the power of God, the Word of God, to shatter, utterly destroy the works of the wicked that wants to destroy us by dividing us through hatred and mistrust of each other.

For too long this has gone on and it must cease and desist right now, and now that we have the revelation, lets move, for God will bring about the manifestation.

Through the spiritual self defense and life preservation strategy of BIBLE CODE 7 we can and will attain critical mass needed to effect this massive change.

I am,

Dr. Norman DaCosta

Prayer

May The Lord grant wisdom and understanding to every reader of this book, may the information conveyed be prayed upon and be incorporated in their lives on a daily basis, may the tender loving mercies of Jesus be upon them and convey them to that final destination in Jesus Christ. May divine acceleration come to them so they can overtake all who started before them and even though late the hour, they will fulfill and complete their God given destinies.

Other Books By Dr. Norman Dacosta

@biblecode7.com
amazon
barnes and nobles
email. drnormandacosta@gmail.com
Completed August 10, 2020

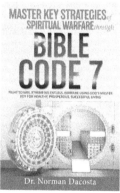
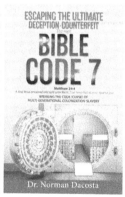

CPSIA information can be obtained
at www.ICGtesting.com
Printed in the USA
LVHW111457190821
695554LV00002B/296